The Fractal Key

Stephen Shaw

The Fractal Key

First published in the United Kingdom in 2016 by Stephen Shaw

Cover art by Deborah Grieves - http://cynnalia.deviantart.com

Publisher and author website and contact details:
www.i-am-stephen-shaw.com

ISBN: 978-0-9928042-5-1

Stephen Shaw's Books

Visit the website: www.i-am-stephen-shaw.com

I Am contains spiritual and mystical teachings from enlightened masters that point the way to love, peace, bliss, freedom and spiritual awakening.

Heart Song takes you on a mystical adventure into creating your reality and manifesting your dreams, and reveals the secrets to attaining a fulfilled and joyful life.

They Walk Among Us is a love story spanning two realities. Explore the mystery of the angels. Discover the secrets of Love Whispering.

The Other Side explores the most fundamental question in each reality. What happens when the physical body dies? Where do you go? Expand your awareness. Journey deep into the Mystery.

Reflections offers mystical words for guidance, meditation and contemplation. Open the book anywhere and unwrap your daily inspiration.

5D is the Fifth Dimension. Discover ethereal doorways hidden in the fabric of space-time. Seek the advanced mystical teachings.

Star Child offers an exciting glimpse into the future on earth. The return of the gods and the advanced mystical teachings. And the ultimate battle of light versus darkness.

The Tribe expounds the joyful creation of new Earth. What happened after the legendary battle of Machu Picchu? What is Christ consciousness? Who are the 144,000?

The Fractal Key reveals the secrets of the shamans. This handbook for psychonauts discloses the techniques and practices used in psychedelic healing and transcendent journeys.

It's my birthday today. 43 years old. And I feel it. Sit up in bed and rub my eyes. Ruffle my hair.

Exhale a big sigh.

Another day at the office. I should be grateful. Well qualified, educated, working in the field I love. Process engineering at Intel Corporation, at their huge site located 25 kilometres west of Portland, Oregon.

I am renting a room in Oak Hills, just a short drive from work. No commuting stress. Recently traded in the car for a Harley-Davidson Road King. Every day I ride past our marital house. Sold it six months ago. Another family has moved in. It cuts my heart.

Why couldn't we make it work? On paper we were so similar – education, socio-economic, cultural, techie-geeks with a love of nature. Yet something was missing. Deep heart connection? The pitter-patter of little feet? Inevitable intense conversations and dissipation of joy. Now we are merely a divorce statistic.

Stroke my unshaven cheek with the back of my hand. Maybe it's time to grow a beard.

You build a life as best you can, using the tools available. You make decisions based on accrued knowledge and life experience.

You follow societal rules and guidelines. You have a moral code and try to be a good person. How does it end like this? How does it go so wrong?

Here I am in a rented room with a handful of possessions. A resplendent motorbike reposes in the garage. My parents passed away a few years ago. I have a sister in California. A couple of close friends. Plenty of savings in my bank account. That's the extent of my life.

Feels quite empty.

I get out of bed and take a long shower. Sometimes it's the highlight of my day. Listen to me! You'd think I was depressed. Scrunch my lips. Stare at the rivulets chasing down the wall. I'm not depressed. Just despondent, disillusioned and disheartened.

Dry myself with a rough towel. Dress in a navy blue suit and white shirt. I have a meeting with the boss today. End of one project. Beginning of another. Go downstairs to the communal kitchen. Grab coffee. Pour granola into a bowl. Add water. Yes, water. Dairy products are laden with lactose and fat. Never cared for alternatives like almond or oat milk. Instead I obtain my bifidobacterium and lactobacillus from a probiotic supplement, and my calcium from green leafy vegetables.

I smile contentedly. At least my health is excellent. The payoff from minimising red meat, eliminating dairy, avoiding sugar and sweeteners, and consuming mostly organic food. And thanks to a religious mother and conservative atheist father, I have never used tobacco or recreational drugs. I do, however, enjoy the occasional beer.

Grab my jacket and helmet. Bluetooth technology transmits GPS directions, phone calls and music directly into the full-face helmet. Optimal protection and pleasure. Riding the Harley is pure joy – my mind ceases thinking and ruminating, my being merges into the present moment, my soul becomes imbued with freedom. It's the ultimate morning meditation.

I walk into the office and my mood shifts. I don't want to be here. What is going on with me? It's a great job and solid reliable company. Yet I feel trapped, constrained, claustrophobic. Can't understand it. Am I having the classic midlife crisis?

I drink a glass of cold water. Must pull myself together. Summoned to the meeting. Handshakes, smiles and congratulations. A steel girder snaps in my mind. A warm tear burns my eye. I hear my voice softly perforating the jubilant atmosphere. "I can't do this anymore. Divorce. Midlife crisis. I don't know. I need a break. Few months away. Unpaid leave. Resignation if necessary."

Weak and pathetic and unprofessional. I will probably be fired. Slump in the leather chair and await my fate.

Surprisingly, the response is empathic and consolatory. Hand on my shoulder. Reassuring smile. An offer of counselling and time off work. I decline the former. A Human Resources manager arrives to discuss leave options. I am between projects and there is workforce flexibility. We agree that I finish the week. From mid-November I will take two weeks' paid vacation followed by three months' unpaid leave.

Express my deepest gratitude. Huge sigh of relief.

Use my spare time shedding what little possessions I have. Prudently and sensibly packing the Harley's two saddlebags. Saying goodbye to colleagues and friends.

Saturday 5.30am. 15 degrees Celsius and rainy. Colder weather on its way. Not sure where I am going. Insouciant shrug. Las Vegas will be sunny and warm.

I point the bike southeast and start the engine.

Just me and the open road.

* * *

I ride Route 26 through Mount Hood National Forest then along 20 and 95 where I cross into Nevada. Clocked at exactly 6 hours. It is 11.30am and the temperature is pleasant. Time to stretch the legs and have a sandwich.

30 minutes later I am on the bike again.

Straight down Route 95. Surrounded by expansive scenery. Sensation of utter freedom. Turn onto Route 80 then 305 and 376. Mountains and pale blue skies. Bliss. Turn east onto Route 6. Check the time: 4pm.

Swoosh! Overtaken by a shimmering bike. Friendly wave.

I ride a little further and pull over at the junction at Warm Springs. Hmm … that's the guy from a few minutes ago. I amble over to him.

"Hey brother. Mind if I join you?"

Hey man. What's good?

Shrug my shoulders.

"Left Oregon 5.30 this morning. Just need a short rest. Headed to Las Vegas. You?"

Left San Francisco at midday. Passing through Las Vegas. Sun goes down in half an hour. You need more than a short rest.

I check out his bike.

"Cool ride. Indian?"

Indian Chief Vintage.

"Nice leather saddlebags."

He nods appreciatively.

There's a motel down the road. At Rachel. With an alien-themed restaurant and bar.

"Alien-themed?"

Yeah, man. Don't you know where you are?

I look around blankly.

We are both going to turn right onto Route 375. In 1996 Route 375 was renamed Extraterrestrial Highway. It runs alongside the north-eastern edge of Area 51. I am savouring the moment.

Laughter grips me.

"I don't believe in that stuff."

What do you believe?

Defeated murmur.

"I don't know anymore."

Follow me to Rachel. Have a burger. Get some sleep.

He flashes me a broad smile.

I tilt my head and gaze at him. African American, solid build, short hair, youthful, good-looking, branded clothes. Feels like a trustworthy guy.

"Yeah, why not? Probably good advice."

We hop on our bikes. Within 40 minutes we arrive at the Little A'Le'Inn motel. The signboard reads 'Earthlings Welcome'. I suppress a giggle.

My companion has reserved a room. Fortunately one is available for me. We stow our bags and meet in the restaurant.

Alien paraphernalia and souvenirs everywhere. The ceiling above the bar is plastered with signed currency from around the world left by UFO seekers. Two guys are arguing about teleportation. The words 'loophole' and 'jump' drift our way. Weird atmosphere.

We settle down and order burgers and fries.

I never introduced myself. Bernard Sanguine.

Shakes my hand firmly and grins.

"Alexander Huxley."

So what's your backstory?

I glance around the restaurant. The two guys have disappeared. We're alone.

"Don't want to bore you."

I'm genuinely interested.

Stroke my newly forming beard and sigh. Succinctly recount losing the woman I love, the pain of divorce, the recent passing away of both parents, and the sudden disinterest in my work.

Sounds like you're hurting.

"I guess."

The waitress places the food on the table.

"What's your name, honey?"

I glance up at her.

"Alexander."

"Wait, don't tell me. 43 years old. Lost your way. Broken heart."

Ouch. That's a bit personal.

"Am I right?"

I nod.

"A woman waits for you. She will call you Sasha. It's a derivative of Alexander. Your name means 'defender of humankind'. You will tread an interesting path."

No one has ever called me Sasha.

"Uh … thank you."

She turns her attention to Bernard who immediately volunteers his full name. Touches her forehead. Closes her eyes.

"Oh dear. A pair of broken hearts I see. Soul brothers who need healing. No coincidence that you met. Bernard means 'brave, strong as a bear' and Sanguine means 'optimistic or positive, especially in a difficult situation'. Very suitable names."

She pats him on the shoulder and smiles.

"Eat up, boys. Before your burgers get cold."

I stare at my food. What just happened?

It's okay, man. Psychic, no doubt.

"Was she right about you?"

Yeah, missed my age though. I'm 25.

Bite into my burger. Oh, that's good.

"How did your heart get broken?"

My father was a heavy drinker. When I was 19 my parents and younger sister were killed in a car accident. He was driving. I was not in the car. Ripped my life apart. Since then I refuse to drive a car and I never touch alcohol. After inheriting the house and life insurance I enrolled in university and earned a degree in anthropology. Had to do something to take my mind off the pain.

"Sorry to hear. Impressive that you managed to study under those circumstances."

Yeah, but I delayed the inevitable. Never dealt with the grief. Never sought counselling. It's all bottled up inside. My girlfriend Crystelle lives with me in my parent's house. She has been very patient and understanding. I struggle with emotional intimacy. I cannot commit. It's like I'm suspended in some dreamworld, drifting among unresolved issues. I negotiated time away to search for healing.

This is turning into a sombre meal.

"Seems we've become lone rangers."

I will combine my quest with a trip to Mexico.

"Why Mexico?"

A strong interest in Mesoamerican history and culture. It was the thesis of my anthropology degree.

I clear my throat.

"Anthropology?"

The study of humans, past and present. Human societies, cultures and their development.

"Aha."

Got space for an interesting personal snippet?

"Instead of dessert?"

Quizzical frown.

"Tell me."

I was named after Bernardino de Sahagun (1499-1590). Even our last names sound similar. Bernardino was a Franciscan friar, missionary priest and pioneering ethnographer in colonial New Spain (now Mexico). He travelled to New Spain in 1529 and spent more than 50 years in the study of Mexica (Aztec) beliefs, culture and history. He compiled the Florentine Codex and his remarkable work earned him the title 'first anthropologist'.

"Interesting coincidence."

The waitress appears and removes our empty plates. She looks Bernard in the eye. "It's called synchronicity. There are no coincidences. Do you believe in reincarnation?"

Before he can answer, she tilts her head and winks at me.

"Alexander, when you have a clear destination, the universe will conspire to support you."

She turns and walks away.

Bernard is smiling.

Do you know where you're going?

"Not really."

Why not come to Mexico?

Purse my lips.

"I'll give it some thought."

Push the chair out. Ruffle my hair.

"Time for a shower and bed. I'm exhausted. See you at breakfast."

Cool, man. What time?

"Whenever I wake up."

Twenty minutes later sleep deftly overtakes me.

* * *

My body has shifted into an early biorhythm. I am standing outside at 6.20am watching yellow-orange rays flickering and cascading across the horizon. Breathing the fresh crisp air. A beautiful start to the day.

All these thoughts rolling through my mind. Where am I going? Do I want a companion on this journey? Who is the peculiar waitress? Will I be responsible for the young man?

We are both hurting. I am slightly jaded and disillusioned about life. He still has that youthful optimism and exuberance.

I am not looking for a father figure.

The voice behind me makes me jump.

"Sheesh! You wearing ninja shoes?"

He smiles gregariously.

Just came to admire the sunrise. Seriously though, I am responsible for my life. I know we have just met. Perhaps you don't want entanglement. You want to ride by yourself, free as the wind.

Sigh deeply. Stare at the ground.

"The waitress was right. Lost my way. I cannot guide or mentor you. I have nothing to offer."

Hey man. Dial it down. We are all learning and growing. You don't have to do it alone. It's your choice. I am going to Mexico. Who knows what will happen? Life is an adventure.

"The similar backstories shook me a bit. I am trying to cope with my stuff."

Openness engenders trust. Be real. Be free.

"Be real. Be free. Has a nice ring to it."

Yeah. And ride together.

Raise my arms, stretch my back.

"Where will we go?"

Follow the road south.

"That's your plan?"

Uh huh.

"The flow of life."

You decided?

I place my hand on his shoulder.

"Okay, Bernard, I'm in."

He claps jubilantly.

Awesome!

The waitress shouts from the kitchen. "You boys want breakfast or you going to stand there all morning?"

I wave amiably. "On our way."

Feel a growing peace. It's good to have some direction.

A few minutes later we are munching contentedly.

There's one thing I want to do before we ride. Will you come with me?

My ears prick up cautiously.

"What?"

Visit the Black Mailbox. Where Mailbox Road meets Extraterrestrial Highway. It's a few kilometres from here. Not even a detour.

I shrug.

"It's on your bucket list?"

Bucket list?

"List of things you have to do before you die."

He nods his head.

Sure. My bucket list.

"You've never heard of a bucket list?"

You've never heard of the Black Mailbox, have you?

I smile grudgingly.

"Alright, tell me."

It's actually a white mailbox. UFO watchers gather there at night because it provides excellent views of the sky over Groom Lake. Mailbox Road also intersects with 51 Road (aka Groom Lake Road) which runs from Extraterrestrial Highway and leads to the main gate of Area 51.

"A road we shall not be travelling down."

The warning signs make you nervous?

"You mean the ones marked 'Restricted Area', 'No Trespassing' and 'Use Of Deadly Force Authorised'?"

The waitress arrives and clears our plates.

"Well done, Alexander. Every step is on the path."

She gazes at Bernard. "Don't do anything silly. What you seek is within not without."

He frowns at her.

Explain your aphorism.

"Tell me in five words. What are you seeking?"

He stammers then goes quiet. The peculiar ambience makes me ponder the question.

Uh … healing … relief … knowledge … insight … wisdom.

She nods and sits down.

"A lot of unusual souls pass through here. You should head to Sonora, Mexico."

I intervene. "What's there?"

Enigmatic twinkle in her eye. "Not what, who."

"Okay, who?"

"The Rainbow Shaman."

"The Rainbow Shaman?"

"Yes. You can't miss him. Heavily built, bit of a tummy. Laughs a lot. Wears manifold bright colours. Feathers in his hair. Like a psychedelic Buddha. An unconventional maverick."

Maverick?

"Unorthodox and independent-minded individual."

Bernard's eyes are dancing.

Shamans work with ancestral spirits to gain information, do healings and counteract negative energy.

I scrunch my lips uncertainly.

The waitress gets up. "If you follow Route 19 south of Tucson, Arizona, you will arrive at the border and cross from Nogales, Arizona to Nogales, Sonora. Then travel south along Route 15 until you reach Sonora, Sonora."

"You mean the town Sonora in the Mexican state of Sonora."

"The very same. Best of luck, boys."

I scrutinise Bernard's excited countenance. Feels like I am being dragged underwater. Why am I apprehensive? The cautions of a religious mother? The fear of the unknown?

What are your thoughts, Alex?

Swallow hard. Scratch my cheek.

Who is that zany waitress? Why do her words ring in my consciousness? 'When you have a clear destination, the universe will conspire to support you.' I have felt lost and alone for a long time. Support would be a wonderful and welcome change. Companionship would be good for me.

What have you got to lose?

Swoosh. There's the zinger.

Glance into his youthful eyes.

"Nothing. Nothing at all."

Shall we track down the shaman?

I nod affably.

"Yeah, let's do it."

Pull out my GPS and check the map.

"Too much riding for one day. Let's visit that mailbox and head to Sedona, Arizona. Stay the night. Then straight through to Sonora, Sonora the next day."

Bernard extends his hand.

Deal.

I shake it and smile.

"Time to rock 'n roll."

We pay our invoices, pack the saddlebags and hit the open road.

The Black Mailbox, which is actually white and bulletproof, is ten minutes away. Apart from a strange vibe, nothing much is happening here. Bernard poses for a couple of photos and uploads them to his social media accounts. Modern technology. It seems we are all connected these days.

Back on Extraterrestrial Highway. Pass 51 Road. At Crystal Springs we turn onto Route 93. Two hours later we stop for a cold drink in Las Vegas. All those twinkling lights and seductive advertisements. Mexico is definitely a better choice.

It's 11am. We're making good time. An idea ripples through my mind.

"Bernard, you ever visited the Grand Canyon?"

Shakes his head.

"On our way. Shall we go?"

Yeah, for sure.

We hop on the bikes and continue south on Route 93 then turn east onto 40 at Kingman. By 3pm we are standing on the edge of the most magnificent piece of natural scenery. Warm sun is soaking into my body. Fresh air is filling my lungs. Surveying the gorgeous landscape. A couple of kayaks flowing along the winding river. Serene hawks and kestrels hovering in a pale blue sky.

I glance at Bernard. His mouth is agape.

"The Grand Canyon is over 400 km long, varies between 16-29 km across and is 1.6 km deep."

Breathtaking ... spectacular ...

"Retrofitting your bucket list?"

Totally.

An hour later we grab a sandwich then head south to Sedona. We arrive at dusk. There are plenty of hotels so getting a room is easy. We decide to share a room to cut costs. It's been a long day with a fair amount of travelling. After dinner we relax in the lounge. We are quite tired. Early night for both of us.

* * *

Over breakfast we discuss the option of sightseeing in Sedona. Bernard is eager to locate the Rainbow Shaman and I am not interested in the New Age spirituality on offer. We decide to press on with the journey to Mexico.

Sunrise is at 7am. As we ride away from Sedona, the huge sandstone formations illuminate in brilliant orange and red. It is sensational and awe-inspiring.

We head south along Route 17 to Phoenix then 10 to Tucson and connect with 19 which takes us to the border at Nogales, Arizona. Here we acquire our Mexico tourist cards, vehicle permits and insurance. As long as our paperwork is in order, and we are not carrying any illegal items or substances, the crossing should be a breeze. Indeed, by midday we are in Nogales, Mexico.

La Roca restaurant is a few minutes down the road. Nestled into a natural cliff face, the restaurant is named after the stone that frames its main dining room. Soon we are enjoying a delicious meal of broiled tenderloin, salmon, avocado salad and guacamole.

I study Bernard's contented face.

"Do you know that Sonora is largely comprised of desert? Your helmet only covers the top of your head. It looks stylish but offers little protection."

Yeah. I was thinking of wrapping a neckerchief over my nose and mouth.

"Sun is going to fry you. Dust in your eyes. I have a spare full-face helmet."

His body language displays minimal interest.

"Did I mention the technology? Both helmets are hooked up with a bike-to-bike communication system and Bluetooth transmission for GPS directions, phone calls and music. The helmets also have excellent airflow."

His eyes light up.

We can talk to each other? And I can listen to my music?

"For sure."

Quiet for a few seconds, then he nods.

Sensible suggestion. I accept your offer.

Feeling of mild relief. Prefer him to be safe.

An hour later we climb onto our bikes and test the helmets. Crystal clear communication. I see his delighted smile through the tinted visor.

"Good decision?"

Definitely.

"The advantage of travelling south during November is the moderate temperatures. Currently a pleasant 19 degrees Celsius. Makes our journey quite comfortable."

And we avoid the stormy season of Mexico.

He pauses.

Are all engineers metric? Where's the Fahrenheit?

"The International System of Units (aka SI or the metric system) is the official system of weights and measures in every country on the planet except USA, Myanmar (Burma) and Liberia. Even NASA uses the metric system. The basic unit of mass in the metric system is the gram, distance is the metre, and temperature is the degree Celsius."

Understood. Americans don't like change.

"Evolution vs revolution."

Shall we hit the road?

"Yeah, let's go."

We ride south along Route 15 then east onto 14 and turn right at Ures. The three-hour journey has left me rather fatigued. The town of Sonora finally comes into view.

4.30pm. One hour until sunset.

"We need to find a hotel."

Not much going on here.

Rubbing my chin.

"Let's head back down the 14 to Hermosillo. It's the capital city of the state of Sonora. Plenty of hotels there. We can stay the night then revisit the town of Sonora in the morning."

Works for me.

Two hours later we are comfortably ensconced in an air-conditioned lounge. We order a couple of non-alcoholic drinks and peruse the restaurant menu. Not sure if I am hungry or if those are butterflies in my tummy.

Bernard animatedly clinks my glass.

Tomorrow we stalk the Rainbow Shaman.

I feign enthusiasm.

"May the consequences be salubrious."

* * *

After a tasty breakfast of sweet potato chorizo hash with eggs and avocado crema we ride along Route 14 to the town of Sonora.

This is going to be awkward. Two gringos on fancy motorbikes speaking rusty Spanish. I can imagine the response.

Cruising slowly through the neighbourhoods, asking questions like "Conoce el Rainbow Shaman?", "Has visto el Rainbow Shaman?", "Sabe donde encontrar el Rainbow Shaman?". The local people mostly ignore us. Some throw peculiar stares or make comments like "Ellos estan locos." I know what that means.

Hope begins to wane. Park the bikes and sit under a tree. Bernard walks across the road to buy two cold drinks. Seconds later a wrinkled old man sidles up to me. In perfect English, he offers to divulge the location of the elusive shaman. On one condition: I do not tell my young companion. I flatly refuse. He places his palms together and walks away. Eccentric. Soon after this, five children in ragged clothes appear before me. I give each of them a few dollar bills. Sharing is caring.

Bernard returns with an icy drink. Sip it slowly and slake my thirst.

A guy in that store offered to tell me how to find the shaman. Provided I leave you behind.

I sit up anxiously.

"Seriously?"

Yeah. Really weird. I said you are my friend. Never desert a friend.

"Thanks bro."

Scratching my eyebrow.

"Wait a minute. A shrivelled old man?"

Tilts his head.

How did you know?

Stand up quickly and look around.

"Same thing happened to me."

Is the shaman playing with us?

"No idea. Maybe it's a test."

What do you want to do?

An angry shout fills the air. "Vete a casa, gringos!" The burly man approaches us. "What are a black-skin and white-skin doing on our land? Take your culture and go home!"

Bernard raises his open palms.

Hey brother. We are colour-blind. All that counts is the essence of a person. Openness, acceptance, non-judgement.

The man stares harshly at us, then his face softens. "Good answer. We value impeccability, altruism and radical respect. You will find the shaman at Rio Yaqui." He pulls out his mobile phone. "I'll let him know you are coming." Turns and walks away.

"Wow. What just happened?"

We passed an impeccability test.

"The shaman is stalking us."

He nods his head pensively.

This path requires courage and humility.

"That's for sure."

I consult the GPS.

"It's a four-hour trip. Let's get started."

He puts on his helmet and stretches.

Deeper into Mexico we go.

Rev the engines. Fly down Route 14 to Hermosillo then south along 15. Arrive in Rio Yaqui at 4pm.

This is what I studied. You interested in a few facts?

"I am open to a succinct lecture."

Rio means 'river' in Spanish and Portuguese. The Yaqui or Yoeme are an indigenous people who inhabit the valley of the Rio Yaqui in the state of Sonora.

"Thank you."

We cruise the neighbourhood of Pueblo Yaqui, passing a large church, grocery store and a few small businesses. Ride east for a few minutes and reach the river. Park the bikes in the shade, remove our helmets and breathe deeply. The river is lined with verdant trees and plants. Ensconced by mountains and bright beautiful sky. Absorbing the tranquil energy into my being.

"How do you like this, bro?"

I glance at Bernard. He is staring into the distance. Follow his gaze. A brightly clad figure is dancing under a tree. Heavily built. Could it be? I swallow hard, suddenly apprehensive.

Unsure what to do. Sensing a serene and otherworldly ambience.

He is slowly walking toward us. I feel immobilised.

The voice is steady and strong. "What do you want?"

Bernard bows respectfully.

Good afternoon, sir. We seek healing, relief, knowledge, insight, wisdom.

He scrutinises our faces for a long while.

"Would you prefer a radical 20-minute journey or meandering 8-hour journey?"

Bernard flicks his eyes toward me. I blink uneasily.

20-minute journey.

"Good choice. I only do radical journeys." Disarming smile. "Sit down. Open your ears. Pay close attention."

We perch on a flat rock at the water's edge.

"The only way to truly heal is to access the higher levels of consciousness, communicate with the beings of light, absorb teachings from the sacred dimensions. This is not a religion. Nor a place of empty rituals, beliefs or ideology. This is a direct experience of the Light or Source."

The Rainbow Shaman waves his mobile phone in the air.

"You are surrounded by television, radio and phone signals, to name just a few, yet you are unable to access their communication without the correct device. For example, if you use a television receiver you will experience audio-visual information and entertainment.

"Similarly, you are surrounded and permeated with the multi-dimensions. These are not places as much as vibrations or radiances of the Light. You are swimming in multitudinous overlapping waves yet you remain unaware of their communication until you retune your innate receiver. The receiver is your consciousness. You retune it by using a catalyst or **fractal key**.

"Fractal keys open the portal to the multi-dimensions. These keys include meditation, prayer, fasting, drumming, dancing, yoga, tantra, shamanism, teacher plants, psychedelics and entheogens.

"Psychedelic means 'mind-manifesting' and entheogen means 'meeting the divine within'. Entheogen is the preferred term as it denotes the sacredness of the journeys. Psychedelics and entheogens retune your awareness to the vast array of multi-dimensional consciousness, to the infinite layers and levels of the Source.

"Why the term 'fractal key'? Fractals are geometric forms. Kaleidoscope of multicoloured patterns. Luminous vortexes, dazzling tunnels, spinning wheels of light. Fractals are infinitely complex yet every fragment contains the whole. The **first stage** of a healing or transcendent journey is often marked by the appearance of enthralling fractals. Ideally, the **breakthrough stage** follows: entry into other dimensions, meeting beings, receiving guidance, piercing insights, energy release, waves of love, ecstasy. As the journey unfolds, you may cry, shout, scream, laugh, shake, sing, dance. The **ultimate stage** is ego dissolution, the dying of self and discovery of Self. Merging with the Light or Source.

"Fractal keys have varying power. Perhaps you diligently meditate. As the years go by, you hope for a spiritual breakthrough sometime in the next decade. I prefer to schedule breakthroughs for a Saturday afternoon." The shaman bursts into laughter. "Why sit on a cushion for ten years when you can get there in an afternoon?"

He gazes directly into my eyes.

"Do you know how beautiful it is when your mind cracks open and Light pours in ... when your heart cracks open and Love pours in ... when the boundaries of your consciousness dissolve and you discover who You really are?"

I have no idea how to respond. Way beyond me.

"Secrets have been hidden for thousands of years within abstruse texts, cryptic rituals, and the inner sanctum of mysterious orders. Gateways to higher consciousness and transcendence have been closely guarded. Portals to the multi-dimensions and beings of light have been astutely concealed. Now the resonance is shifting. Shamans, spiritual teachers, enlightened guides, extraterrestrial entities and other-dimensional beings are revealing the truth. It's time to set yourself free."

The shaman stands up and smiles.

"When you are ready, you know where to find me."

I look at Bernard's entranced face. The message has touched him deeply. My brow furrows. There are many questions. I cough lightly and turn my head.

The Rainbow Shaman has disappeared.

* * *

I slept deeply. Must be all the travelling. We were fortunate to find a guest house late yesterday evening. Local family with a sizeable spare room, separate beds, and the promise of two hearty meals per day. It will do just fine.

After breakfast we take a walk along the streets.

Bernard is his usual enthusiastic self. I am slightly reticent.

Dude, we have to try these journeys. You felt the shaman's presence and power. And he came recommended.

"You mean by a zany waitress."

She was more than a waitress. You know that. I think it's all connected.

"I'm a bit nervous of psychedelics. Lived such a straight life."

Recreational drugs are harmful to self and others. You didn't miss anything. Shamans only use products that originate from nature.

"Feel strait-jacketed by my upbringing. Religious mother. Conservative father."

Your engineer's brain wants a map with clear parameters.

"Insightful."

Sometimes you have to take a leap of faith.

"Nothing bothers you?"

My parents were religious too. But they always encouraged a seeking mind. They ingrained a motto in me: 'Experience before ideology'. You don't blindly follow a holy teaching or book. Instead you remain open to diverse concepts and ideas and try to discover the truth for yourself.

Swoosh. A zinger to my mind.

"Religion generates copious amounts of faith and fear."

Faith is for people who don't have direct experience of God. Faith desperately props up ideology. Fear stems from facing the unknown. Most people bury their fear or hide it behind faith. Both faith and fear are annihilated by direct experience of God.

"Wow. Where did that come from?"

I feel the shaman's energy upon me. The words tumbled out my mouth.

Surreal atmosphere. Strange sensations.

"The Rainbow Shaman is calling us."

He places his hand on my shoulder.

Bro, let's take a leap into the unknown.

Deep sigh. Slow reflective nod.

"Time to dispel faith and fear."

We walk back, hop on the bikes and head to the river.

There under the same tree is the dancing shaman.

He waves and shouts jovially, "You ready to become psychonauts?"

We stroll over to his location.

Good morning, sir. Psycho-?

"Psyche means 'soul' or 'spirit' or 'mind' and nautes means 'sailor' or 'navigator'. Psychonautics refers to activities that induce and utilise altered states of consciousness (aka ASCs) for spiritual and existential exploration. A person who uses altered states for such purposes is known as a **psychonaut**."

Bernard gives a friendly salute.

Psychonauts reporting for duty.

"You guys been vetted?"

Uh, no sir.

"You may not embark on this entheogen journey if you have a heart condition or if you have high blood pressure or if you are prone to epilepsy or seizures or asthma or if you are under the influence of drugs including marijuana or if you are under the influence of medication including antibiotics and antidepressants and antihistamines or if you are experiencing severe mental or physical health challenges for example schizophrenia or bipolar disorder. You also need to be free of alcohol and caffeine."

Clear and ready, sir.

I mumble my compliance.

"Park yourselves on that flat rock. Listen carefully."

This is obviously important. Better focus my attention.

"**DMT** is a powerful **entheogen** that cracks open human consciousness and exposes your precious beliefs, stories and ideologies to ultimate Love and Light. DMT uncovers the layers of the self. It opens the door to higher knowledge and wisdom. Provides access to the multi-dimensions and beings of light. Melts existential fear. Sets you free.

"DMT or **dimethyltryptamine** is widely distributed throughout the plant and animal kingdoms. It is a naturally occurring chemical found in mammals, marine animals, toads, frogs, mushrooms, barks, grasses, flowers and roots. DMT is molecularly similar to the fungal psychedelic psilocybin (aka magic mushrooms) and the human neurotransmitter serotonin (aka 5-hydroxytryptamine). Human brains synthesise and secrete endogenous DMT. When naturally occurring levels of DMT in the brain are raised above a certain threshold (due to events like physical death or ingestion of an entheogen) radical spiritual and psychological experiences ensue.

"When Amazonian Indians drink the psychoactive brew **ayahuasca** (a blend of the MAO-inhibiting vine *Banisteriopsis caapi* and DMT-laden leafy plant *Psychotria viridis* or *Diplopterys cabrerana*) they undergo a dramatic 4-6 hour psychedelic journey. This often involves intermittent vomiting which shamans say is the release of negative energy. Typical experiences include revealing of buried traumas and shadows, catharsis, a feeling of dying, encounters with higher beings, beautiful visions, deep teachings and profound insights.

"Tukano shamans of the Columbian Amazon create a potent psychoactive snuff they call **viho** from the dark red resin of *Virola* tree bark. The resin contains several psychedelic alkaloids, notably three powerful members of the DMT family: **5-MeO-DMT** (5-methoxy-*N,N*-dimethyltryptamine), ***N,N*-DMT** (*N,N*-Dimethyltryptamine) and **bufotenin**; it also contains beta-carboline harmala alkaloids, MAO inhibitors that greatly potentiate the effects of DMT. The snuff is blown through a long pipe into the nostrils by an assistant. Viho is very short-acting, lasting no more than 5 minutes, with no negative effects. The shamans say that viho is the principal way to contact the spirit beings in the higher realms.

"*Mimosa tenuiflora* (aka *Mimosa hostilis*) root bark and *Acacia simplicifolia* (aka *Acacia simplex*) bark can be treated and processed to extract *N,N*-DMT. The resultant crystals are usually vaporised and inhaled in a few successive breaths. Onset after inhalation is very fast (less than 45 seconds). Effects last for 5-15 minutes. The journey includes beautiful visuals, large influxes of energy, and interactions with advanced beings (often initially disguised as fairies, elves, jokers, clowns, snakes, spiders, mantises, bees, animals, hybrid animals or stick figures). The experience occasionally feels like an interaction with a cosmic computer program. The body builds a fast tolerance to smoked DMT so you cannot engage in immediate consecutive sessions. There are no negative effects.

"And finally, there is my speciality: **Mystic Toad**.

"The Sonoran Desert Toad or Colorado River Toad (*Bufo alvarius*) is usually found in the lower Colorado River and Gila River catchment areas in south-eastern California, southern Arizona, New Mexico and Mexico. It is the largest native toad in the United States and can grow up to 19 centimetres long. It is nocturnal and semi-aquatic.

"The *Bufo alvarius* toad contains large amounts of the potent entheogen 5-MeO-DMT in specialised glands on its neck and limbs. The 5-MeO is gently milked, dried, vaporised by heat and taken into the lungs in the form of smoke. It produces an incredibly intense psychedelic experience lasting 3-5 minutes followed by a gradual return to normal consciousness. The entire journey lasts about 20 minutes. 5-MeO rockets you through the multi-dimensions and immerses you into the Source or Light. There is no time to meet beings or receive teachings. Ego and fears are blown away. The experience is overwhelming, shifting you into euphoric 'wows' and mind-shattering bliss. The journey is not for the faint-hearted."

I shift uneasily on the hard surface.

Bernard studies the shaman.

Why bypass beings of light and higher teachings?

Enlightened smile.

"To meet God. To immerse in the Light."

We are both quiet for a while. Feels like a huge decision.

I stretch my back, take a deep breath, nod my head. "I'm ready."

Awesome, bro! Let's turn the fractal key.

The Rainbow Shaman raises his hands.

"Two things you need to consider."

Yes?

"**Readiness** and **resistance**. These occur on two levels: conscious and unconscious. Clearly you are both consciously ready. However, you may have hidden resistance. This arises primarily from unconscious fear, which in turn stems from your psychological makeup, childhood experiences and unresolved past life traumas.

"Remember the three **crucial navigation tools**: **witness**, **breathe**, **surrender**. If you feel fearful or overwhelmed take a deep breath and watch what is happening. Try to welcome the experience and surrender. These are, of course, the techniques you learn from meditation, particularly mindfulness meditation."

Have to admit the shaman is very knowledgeable. I had expected a simple man-of-the-earth. Instead he seems to be an expert in his field. His exemplary English and detailed teachings have engendered a feeling of confidence. I volunteer to do the first journey.

He beckons us to sit on a large blanket under his tree.

I notice the twinkle in his eye.

"You have entered a sacred space. This shamanic circle will keep you safe and protected. I am lighting a stick of Palo Santo (aka holy wood) to waft the smoke around you and clear your energy. It's always a good practice before commencing a sacred journey."

He motions Bernard to step off the blanket. The focus is now on me.

"I will apply a flame to the 5-MeO crystals in this glass pipe. You need to fully exhale then put your lips to the pipe and fully inhale. Hold the smoke in your lungs as long as possible."

There is a moment of anxiety. He lights the pipe. I exhale then breathe in the white vapour. Hold it ... hold it ... Feel my body fall backward. Swirl of smoke escapes my lungs. Intensely bright fractal spinning before me. Covering my entire visual field. Is it coming toward me or I am moving toward it? Suddenly engulfs me like a cosmic shock wave. "Wow." Here comes another, with even more vigorous energy. Whoosh! "Oh my God!" Witness. Surrender. The waves are speeding up. Each wave is more intense. "Aaargghh!" My arms and legs are flailing wildly. I can't control this. Fear wells up. Breathe. I am screaming and screaming. Light is trying to overwhelm me. Am I dying? The waves begin to subside. My body becomes still. Vague sense of loving presences. Is someone talking to me? Unable to move. Drifting away.

Fifteen minutes later I blink and open my eyes. The shaman is gazing tenderly at me. "You are safe. Everything is fine. Welcome back."

Sit up and rub my temples. "Wow. That was crazy. What happened?"

He laughs knowingly. "Unconscious fear. Resistance. Survival instinct. Your body thought it was going to die. The boundaries of your ego were under threat. It can be terrifying."

I glance at Bernard. Has my journey made him anxious?

How are you feeling, Alex?

"It's awesome and incredible and scary."

I was worried about you.

"Way beyond everyday experience. Freaked my mind."

The shaman places his hand on my shoulder. "You are a fighter. A survivor. You don't easily surrender. It's a lesson you need to learn."

Nod my head solemnly. My entire life has been a battle. Not enough support. Alone in the corner. Achieving against the odds. Constant challenges. Distinct lack of joy.

I stumble off the blanket.

"Your turn, brother."

Bernard takes centre-stage, sitting down in a meditative position. Asks for a few minutes of silence. Is he praying? Settling his mind? Need to respect his quiet strategy.

Signals his readiness. Exhale. Deep inhale. Falls backward. Unmoving. Wordless. Eventually one soft "Wow." Rises onto his hands and knees. Crawls a few metres. Rolling on the ground, humming and laughing. Now on his feet, arms above his head, peculiar symmetrical movements, like the dance of an exotic god.

After twenty minutes he opens his eyes.

Hey dude. What's up?

"Share your experience?"

Shrugs peacefully.

Colossal waves of pulsing light. Drawing me deeper. All I remember.

"See where you are?"

Yeah. How did I get here?

I describe his actions. He is incredulous.

We look at the shaman for an explanation.

Inscrutable smile. "Your body was flowing with divine energy. When you have few barriers, the Source cascades through your being."

Half an hour later Bernard is back to full strength. We are informed that only one journey per day is permissible. We pay him for his services and express our gratitude. He invites us to return whenever we are ready.

We mount the bikes and go for a long ride. Perhaps it will take the edge off our wild experiences. A psychedelic shaman and a mystic toad. The extraordinary morning has left us much to ponder.

* * *

We both wake exhilarated and full of energy. It's chilaquiles for breakfast, crunchy tortillas covered in sauce, along with refried beans, eggs and salsa.

"I'm feeling excellent. Some sort of transition."

Yeah. Hard to define. Effortless … fluid … free.

"Catapulted into God and the only resistance is you."

Entire universe loaded into a cannon and fired into your mind.

I smile approvingly.

"Accurate analogy."

The Light cannot fully enter if there are rigid boundaries.

"Hmm. Overprotected cores. Sensitive egos."

Impossible to completely resist. Total onslaught on barriers.

"Cosmic stones that eventually crack a windscreen."

Perhaps if we repeat 5-MeO more Light will get through.

"It's kind of a rough way to heal."

Bernard laughs gleefully.

Direct non-negotiable experience of the Source.

"Courage and humility required."

Shall we go to the river after breakfast?

"Yep. Once the food settles."

Awesome.

By mid-morning we are parked near the sacred tree.

The Rainbow Shaman greets us merrily.

"Come, come, you must try this."

He demonstrates rhythmic movements.

What are you doing?

"The dance of the deer. It celebrates our relationship with nature."

For the next hour we are prancing along the water's edge. As my analytical mind quietens, it becomes kind of fun.

"The uninhibited flow of life, my friends."

We finally sit on the blanket. His face creases into a broad smile.

"Any questions before your journeys?"

A little clarity about the 5-MeO experience.

"Your consciousness is rocketed through the layers and levels of the Source. Onward and upward. As much as you can handle. In simple terms, it is the destruction of the self and the discovery of the Self."

And those pulsing waves?

"Higher dimensions. Radiances of the Light."

So we are hurtling toward the Light.

"Melting into higher radiances means little deaths of self. This may be scary. And exhilarating. It's the 5-MeO way. The direct path. Ecstatic and unstoppable. You shout or scream if you have barriers resulting from unconscious fears, wounds or traumas. However, it is simply the breaking of self as you move through each level on the way to the Source. It can be overwhelming, terrifying and blissful to meet the *mysterium tremendum* or 'awe-inspiring mystery'. Your relatively tiny point of consciousness is merging with the Origin, the underlying Is-ness, the infinite Consciousness."

The direct path is radical and intense.

"Most people choose to encounter God slowly, in stages, over many journeys. Usually through more sedate fractal keys, for example meditation or subtler entheogens."

Twenty years on a cushion.

"Or twenty lifetimes."

And all those rituals.

The shaman winks at Bernard.

"I'm into experience not ideology."

He stares in surprise then avidly agrees.

Absolutely. Shall we journey now?

I suggest that Bernard goes first. He reposes on the blanket with eyes closed. Soon he sits up and the shaman lights the glass pipe. Deep breath. Falls backward. Then moves onto his elbows and knees, hunched down like a toad, head resting on hands. It appears to be a worship posture. Suddenly he raises his arms to the sky and shouts "It's all in my mind!"

Twenty minutes later he opens his eyes and looks at me.

That's wild, man.

"What happened?"

Laying on my back, being engulfed by those waves, made me feel vulnerable. I shifted my body position and it changed the perspective. Instead I was looking down the vortex. Slipped into it like a surfer. As I thought about different colours, the vortex altered into various hues and tints. Somehow my mind was influencing my reality.

He blinks a few times.

I am creating my reality.

"Profound insight."

Hmm. Gives rise to more questions.

The sky is shimmering through the leafy treetops. Although Sonora is generally mountainous and arid, the area along the river is lush and green. The tranquillity of nature coalescing with the shaman's esoteric energy creates a surreal atmosphere.

Eventually Bernard hops off the blanket.

I swallow apprehensively. Hope I don't scream.

Here we go. Exhale. Full inhale. Hold it. Hold it. Fall onto my back. Oh my God. It's so intense. Trying to get up, control it. A being reaching out to me. Anthropomorphic light telling me it's okay, relax, you're safe. Focus on breathing. There's less fear. 'You are not you.' Strange voice. Waves expanding toward me. Overlapping. Engulfing. "Wow, wow, wow!"

Then it moderates. Can't move my body. 'Say goodbye to your mother.' Tears rolling down my cheeks. Sense her energy. Her potent grip on me. The fear drizzling within my soul. 'Say goodbye.' Unable to find the strength. Tiny feet dancing all around me, a troupe of resolute elves. Tapping becomes louder and louder. Feel like I am going to vomit. Everything abates.

Open my eyes. Shake my head. Struggle to speak.

The shaman moves closer to me.

"A dark energy haunts you. You will have to face it. Then let it go."

Sombre sigh. "Yeah, but not today."

I stand up and trudge toward my bike. Must get out of here. Need some space. Climb on, rev the engine, drift through town, disappear onto the highway.

Two hours later I head back to the river. I should apologise to the shaman. To my surprise, Bernard is sitting alone on the flat rock.

"Hey bro. What are you doing?"

Waiting for you.

"Really?"

Checks his watch.

Yep. Shaman said you would return right about now.

"Seriously?"

Uncanny prediction.

"Sorry about deserting you."

No worries, man. Shaman said you needed space to process.

"Is he around?"

Running some errands.

"Oh."

It's all cool. He understands.

"You're probably right."

I extend my hand.

"Buy you some lunch?"

He smiles effervescently.

Thought you'd never ask.

We find a place offering juicy steaks. Craving a beer. The journey rules take precedence, however, and I am mindful about Bernard's attitude to alcohol. Especially after I abandoned him.

He clinks my cold drink glass.

This is why we came here, bro.

I look at him quizzically.

Healing, relief, knowledge, insight, wisdom.

"You speak the truth."

I clink his glass in return.

"Thanks for being my friend."

We are travelling this road together.

I stare into the sky and nod.

"For sure, brother."

Life is a journey. It's going to be alright.

* * *

I am up early in the morning. Couldn't sleep. My dreams were frightening. In a hippy camper van with my closest friends. Accidentally drive off a cliff. Falling vertically into a deep expansive lake. Desperately trying to escape as water fills the van. Vaguely sensing a peaceful imminence yet fighting for my life.

Bernard, on the other hand, slept very well.

My grumpy face keeps our conversation to a minimum. He is probably also keeping his distance because of yesterday. Fortunately breakfast is light – homemade chipotle and jalapeno bagels – otherwise I'd be pushing my food around the plate.

It's a relief to hop on the bikes and ride to the river. Hopefully today will be more pleasant.

The shaman motions us to sit on his huge blanket. It is wide enough to easily lay five people next to each other. Never noticed the design before. Perhaps I was too nervous. Two beautiful stallions galloping side by side against a blue-grey background of winter trees. The material is thick and plush, inviting one to curl up and get cosy.

"It is a San Marcos blanket. Latinos have a special bond with their colourful cobijas. They symbolise comfort and home."

I nod appreciatively.

Once we are settled I discuss my dream with the shaman.

He smiles compassionately.

"The water represents the Source. You desire to be immersed in the Source yet you fear it. This relates to the issue of surrender vs survival. On a more personal note it connects to a past life trauma. However, you can only process such trauma when your soul is ready."

Great. That tells me nothing.

What do you mean by 'soul'?

"It is merely a colloquialism employed to facilitate understanding. Everyday language is useful when dealing with caterpillars. Butterfly language will confuse you. You are a **point of consciousness**. Some people prefer the term 'soul'. The Sun is shining infinite rays of light. You are a point on one of those rays of light. Your position dictates your perception which dictates your reality. If you shift your awareness, in other words move along your particular ray, you will discover things currently hidden from you. In more advanced work, you can jump onto other rays."

Is that butterfly language?

The shaman swiftly smacks Bernard between the shoulder blades.

Oh my God. Where are we? Where's Alexander?

"Beautiful, yes?"

What's going on?

"A dimension coexisting with Earth reality."

How did I get here?

"I shifted your assemblage point. Your awareness is now further along the ray of light."

Take me back. Alexander will be concerned.

"We are manifesting in both dimensions. He can still see us."

Take me back.

The shaman strikes Bernard again.

Wow. That was insane.

Takes a deep breath.

How many worlds are there?

"Grains of sand on a beach. Stars in the sky."

Bernard looks across at me.

Could you see the other world?

Shake my head. No idea what's happening.

You need to journey first. That has blown my mind.

"No worries. Take a time out."

Close my eyes and try to calm myself. Imagine taking a cool shower on a warm Caribbean beach. In the shimmering distance walks a beautiful figure. Slowly approaching me. A gorgeous pink flower in her long dark hair. The flower's symmetrical petals give it the appearance of a fractal wave. The woman beckons me with her soft hand. "I am waiting for you."

Open my eyes and snap out of it. Phew. That was so real. A daydream out of control.

The shaman is gently studying my face.

"The flower is *Dahlia pinnata,* the national flower of Mexico. And that was no daydream."

"Wha-a-a-t?"

"You ready for your journey?"

"I guess."

He loads the glass pipe and lights the flame. Exhale. Big inhale. Hold it. Hold it. Onto my back. Hands tremoring. Body settles. Sense of bright loving arms welcoming me. Onset of enormous fractal waves. Falling into a brilliant dahlia flower comprised of pure light with faint outlines. Rushing *scchhh!* sound. An ethereal disc grinder is sanding down my rough edges. Are these my barriers? Wave of ecstasy hits me. Whoosh! Then another and another. "Oh my God!" Is my soul going to orgasm? Overwhelming ... intense ... can't cope ... too much.

My consciousness returns. I am leaning back against the tree. My face feels strange. Have I been laughing? Wow, the leaves are alive ... fluttering ... in loving correspondence with the branches. Shifting my gaze. My goodness. The river is nurturing many life forms ... insects ... birds ... fish ... plants. Nature is a swirling network of serene energy. It's all connected. Amazing.

Hey Alex.

"Hey brother."

I reach my arms out.

"Come here."

Give him a big hug.

"Love you, man."

He shifts uncomfortably. I let him go.

Good journey?

"Yeah. Bit of a breakthrough."

That's awesome. Well done.

Shake the cobwebs from my brain. Roll off the blanket.

"Over to you, bro. Enjoy."

Perhaps because of his athleticism or youth, one minute after inhaling, Bernard jumps to his feet and starts running through the trees. The shaman dashes after him. I am still too dazed to get up. A flamboyant shaman is chasing a tripping young stallion. Giggles begin to ripple through me. Twigs are crackling, branches swinging, eventually a big splash. Five minutes later two soaked aliens saunter toward me. Gripping my sides with laughter.

Bernard glares at me.

Not funny, dude.

The shaman stands him in the sun away from his cherished blanket.

Desperately try to suppress a giggle. After a while the shock wears off and we are all laughing.

Bernard shakes his head.

What was that all about?

The shaman clasps his hands. "The Mystic Toad is reflecting your issues. When your wounds arise, three outcomes are possible: **fight, flight or deal**. You took flight."

Another round of raucous laughter.

Bernard strokes his scalp.

Please explain more.

"Wounds, traumas and issues are buried for a reason. Usually too painful to acknowledge or explore. May be suppressed for years or decades or lifetimes. When the traumatic energy arises it often triggers intense fear. That is one reason why people have panic attacks. Alex is adept at fighting, controlling, surviving, which has resulted in rigid boundaries. Bernard is skilled at emotional safety, distance and flight, which has created problems with intimacy and connection."

Ouch. The truth is a blunt knife.

"When you are ready, you will face your issues and deal with them."

How can we be ready?

"Psychedelic journeys soften your rough edges and wear down your barriers. They simultaneously surface your issues and saturate you with deep insight, love and euphoria. The process is always controlled by your readiness and resistance. Therefore you deal with issues in your own time, at your own pace. Journeys tend to be 70% comfortable, 30% challenging, a sagacious mix that results in optimal healing and transcendence."

What is your best advice?

"Trust the process."

Understood.

"And use your navigation tools."

Witness, breathe, surrender.

The shaman sighs contentedly.

"My work here is done."

He gives a friendly salute.

"See you guys tomorrow."

Ah. Guess that's our cue.

Bernard places his palms together and bows.

We thank him profusely, make payment and clamber onto our bikes.

A delicious lunch is in order. I feel like celebrating.

* * *

The new day dawns. Warm sun peeks through the window. Light-hearted smile tiptoes across my face. Languid yawn, buoyant stretch. I feel fabulous!

"Hey sleepyhead."

What's up, man?

"How you doing this morning?"

A little despondent.

"Need a cuddle?"

A pillow hurtles toward me.

Dude, seriously.

Raise my palms.

"Just kidding."

Going to shower. See you at breakfast.

Hmm. Gentle approach advisable.

Half an hour later we are seated before bowls of quinoa topped with avocado slices, fried eggs, salsa and fresh cilantro. Season with a little salt and pepper. Yummy.

"Sorry, bro. You had a tough time yesterday."

Never thought I'd have to face my shadow.

"Shadow?"

The stuff that is buried deep. Hidden from conscious awareness.

"That's what made you take flight?"

Yeah, dude.

"Healing is dealing."

Apparently.

"5-MeO turns you upside down and inside out."

Shakes you radically.

"Sees what falls out."

We burst into laughter.

Let's hope we survive.

Push my bowl aside.

"Ready for another round?"

Frowns and rubs his shoulders.

The shaman's probably expecting us.

"We can take the long way. No rush."

That's kind of the point, isn't it?

"Huh?"

The Mystic Toad is the shortest way.

"Direct route to healing."

Precisely.

We cruise through the streets for a while then head to the river.

Another day of dancing with the Light.

The shaman is frantically waving and shouting.

"Come on, come on. You are going to miss it."

We park our bikes and chase after him.

He is crouching by the water's edge.

"Do you see it?"

Wow. The Mystic Toad.

"Beautiful, yes?"

It's huge ... olive-green skin with regular brown spots ... large puffy glands behind the eyes ... more glands on the limbs ... sensation of unperturbed power ... seems to know it carries a potent entheogen ... a placid god of the river.

"He chose to reveal himself to you."

The toad is nocturnal, right?

"Exactly. You are blessed."

Bernard is elated and enrapt.

Have to admit, this is ultra-cool.

After a few minutes it hops away.

The shaman clasps his hands furtively.

"Right, boys, let's get to work."

Moment of anxiety.

Ok if I go first today?

"Suits me, bro."

Bernard reposes on the plush cobija. Closes his eyes. Takes a few deep breaths. Then sits up with a serious countenance. Nods. The shaman flames the 5-MeO crystals. Within seconds my friend is flat on his back. Unmoving. Soundless.

Still nothing. What is occurring?

Twenty minutes later he stirs. Slow blink. Genial smile. Raises his hand unsteadily for a high five. We slap our palms together. Give him a few moments. Eventually he props onto an elbow.

Shakes his head slowly.

Dude, I went home.

"Home?"

Sheepish grin.

Yeah.

Points to the sky.

Faraway planet. Advanced race.

"Wha-a-a-t?"

Star seed.

I frown incredulously at the shaman.

Exquisite architecture. No war, no poverty.

He sighs deeply.

What are we doing to this planet? Earth is hurting.

Claps his hands loudly.

Time for an intervention!

He looks at the Rainbow Shaman.

You are one of us. You know!

What is going on here?

Bernard suddenly appears agitated.

I'm going to walk among the trees. Need some time alone.

The shaman concurs then invites me onto the blanket.

Rub my tummy. Butterflies are flitting. Deep breaths. Try to relax. Give the signal. Deep exhale. Inhale the white vapour. Hold it. Surrounded by luminescent fractals. Engulfed. Struggle to my feet. I can stand up! Wading in the intense energy. Omnipotent presence encouraging my baby steps. 'Come to me ... come closer.' I am approaching a cosmic father. He loves me. He loves me! 'You are not alone, my son ... never were, never are, never will be. I am always with you, whispering, guiding, hinting the way. You are greatly loved.'

I burst into tears ... heart feels warm ... soul is nurtured.

Overwhelming raptures of Love and Light.

Firm hand on my shoulder.

Step away from the water.

Open my eyes.

"Bernard?"

Here for you.

"What? How?"

It's ok. Everything is cool.

Disoriented. Other world fading. Trees shining brightly. River gurgling merrily. Enchanted by the dabbling duck.

I hear the shaman's chuckle. "It's a Blue-winged Teal. He is greatly loved too."

It takes a while before I settle back into Earth reality. Profound and wonderful experience. Can't fit it into my ideology. Guess my ideology is about to be shattered and rebuilt.

We spend two more hours at the river. No one is talking. Words seem superfluous. Blissful feeling of oneness ... water ... leaves ... trees ... birds ... humans ... sky ... sun ... the beyond. Something magical is happening. And I don't want it to end.

* * *

Awake before dawn. The energy in the room is palpable. Both of us are gripped with enthusiasm and anticipation. We stroll outside to watch the enchanting sunrise. Twenty minutes later we shower and head to breakfast.

Steaming burritos await us. Crammed with potatoes, vegetables, chorizo, sausage, rice, beans and egg. Hot sauce is optional. Perfect fuel for an exciting day.

Mmm ... fully charged. Bring it on!

"I don't understand the events of yesterday."

Perhaps our consciousness is limited.

"Meaning?"

Our position on the ray of light.

"Dictates our perception."

Consequently creates our reality.

"We are not just healing, are we?"

The journeys comprise healing and transcendence.

"Partially beyond comprehension."

I am trying to use the navigation tools.

"Witness, breathe, surrender?"

Yeah. After a journey my mind tries to wrestle with the experience, which often results in confusion and distress. Until the boundaries of my knowledge shift and expand, it seems easier to simply witness, breathe and surrender.

Shaking my head.

"You have wisdom beyond your years."

My body may be young; perhaps my soul is old.

"Touché, my friend."

These journeys are unpredictable.

"Positive intentions. No expectations."

Nice one. Plenty of wisdom in you too.

"Thanks, brother."

Shall we visit the shaman today?

"You're kidding, right?"

A ripple of laughter.

Yeah, bro. Ready when you are.

We hop on our bikes, race to the river, park in the shade.

Survey the locale. Seems eerily quiet.

The San Marcos blanket is missing.

Amble to the water's edge. Crouch, dip my fingers.

Where is the Rainbow Shaman?

Familiar *scchhh!* sound. Shimmering light a few metres away.

We dash toward the glowing ocotillo cactus.

What on earth is happening here?

Shaman's possessions on the ground.

Hairs on my arms standing up.

"Buenos días, amigos. Sorry I'm late."

Whirl around. Brilliant and psychedelic.

Bernard looks as surprised as me.

Where did you come from?

Inscrutable smile.

"You know the answer."

Gestures toward the cactus.

"Grab my blanket. Unfurl it under my tree."

Bernard jumps to the task.

We stride to the sacred location.

Consorting with the shaman creates more questions than answers.

I notice he is staring pointedly at me. Tilts his head. "You're first today."

Try to settle myself. Deep breaths. Relax the shoulders. Here we go again. Lights the flame. Big inhale. Hold it. Boom! Instantly on my feet. Potent energy coursing through my body. Zero control. Moving rhythmically … self disappearing … sensual goddess … four arms swaying in a celestial dance … 'Time for change … destroy and rebuild … move forward' … Feminine and passionate and powerful … swirling through mesquite and ironwood trees … cavorting with desert sunflowers … playing with evening primroses …

I notice Bernard's exuberant face. Oh, my eyes are open. Two worlds intermingling. Ecstatically beautiful. Are these the multi-dimensions? All here now. My arm flows toward my friend. Touch his shoulder lightly. Flourish my hand over the blanket. "All yours. Enjoy the journey."

The shaman waits for my complete return to Earth. Guess we can't have two horses tripping among the flowers. I rein in my joviality and shift into supportive mode.

Bernard centres himself on the blanket. Closes his eyes. Prepares his mind. Shaman offers the glass pipe, enflames the mystic crystals. Huge inhale. Falls onto his back. Body tremoring. I see his hand reaching upward. A turning motion with his fingers. Deep exhale. Motionless for a long while. Stirring … sighing … sitting up …. leaning against the tree.

Hey man.

"You good?"

Met a radiant being. Showed me a door.

"Aha."

Asked me if I'm ready to face my issues.

"Your issues?"

Unconscious stuff. Deep journeys required.

"Explore the basement of your mind?"

Yeah. Surface it. Deal with it.

"Did you open the door?"

Turned the handle. Peeked inside.

"Okay."

Need lengthy visits.

"Understood."

Can I have a hug?

"Are you sure?"

Yeah, I need it.

Embrace him tenderly and briefly.

Thanks, brother.

The shaman seats us both on the blanket. Studious gaze.

"Did you notice a pattern in your last journeys?"

Hmm ... 'time for change ... move forward'.

Bernard bites his bottom lip thoughtfully.

I need longer journeys. Much work to do.

Shaman nods his head in assent.

"The Mystic Toad is departing."

Forlornness creeps over me.

What happens next?

"Travel together. Your paths are entwined."

How do we progress?

"You have glimpsed the Light and cracked open a few barriers and boundaries. You now require slower journeys, deep healing and lesson learning."

Where do we go?

"To the Mazatec."

The Mazatec?

"The Mazatec are an indigenous people who inhabit a mountainous area known as the Sierra Mazateca in the northern part of the state of Oaxaca (*pronounced Wa-ha-ka*). Some communities are also located in the adjacent states of Puebla and Veracruz. The Sierra Mazateca is part of the Sierra Madre de

Oaxaca mountain range and is named after the Mazatec people. The main towns of the Sierra Mazateca are Eloxochitlan de Flores Magon, Huautla de Jimenez and Jalapa de Diaz. Mazatec is a Nahuatl word meaning 'people of the deer'.

"Mazatec shamans use entheogens to facilitate special states of consciousness through which they contact the spirit world and perform healings, cleansings and divinations. Their preferred entheogens are psychoactive Ololiuqui (*Turbina corymbosa* aka *Rivea corymbosa*), psilocybin mushrooms (*Psilocybe mexicana* and *Psilocybe semperviva*) and leaves of the Salvia plant (*Salvia divinorum*). Mazatec shamans are secretive and protective of their knowledge."

Wow. I feel excited and fearful at the same time.

Bernard's face is lit up like a Christmas tree.

The voice deepens and becomes stern.

"Heed my cautions. Those powerful shaman-sorcerers tread the Path of the Spiritual Warrior. Once you open that door, your sword and shield consist of impeccability, altruism and radical respect. A few have strayed from the path of light and become enmeshed in the dark side."

What do you mean?

"There are many worlds beyond this one. Multitudinous dimensions. Infinite possibilities. Your mission is to follow the rays of light and go Home. As you proceed up the Sacred Ladder, you will occasionally encounter dark beings who tempt you with alluring propositions. Beware. The nature of the dark side is conceit, deceit and disconnection. It takes you further and further from the Source until the agony becomes excruciating. And it's a long road back."

Consider us warned.

"The secret is to align yourself with the beings of light that exist in the multi-dimensions. Walk with impeccability, altruism and radical respect. Do no harm and accept no harm. Always journey with an experienced shaman who will naturally protect you. Heal your pain and fear."

A recipe for optimal navigation of the rays of light.

He smiles proudly at Bernard.

"Indeed."

Can you recommend a Mazatec shaman?

Nods shrewdly.

"The Crystal Shaman. A powerful shaman totally committed to the Light. You will find him in Eloxochitlan de Flores Magon. I'll let him know you are coming."

He slowly stands up. There is goodbye in his body language. Opens his arms, invites us into an engulfing bear hug.

We express our gratitude for his time and wise guidance.

Moment of hesitation.

Any final advice?

He stares solemnly at us.

"Abstain from alcohol, nicotine, caffeine."

That's a promise.

"Remember the motto."

Experience before ideology.

"Exactly."

Bernard places his palms together and bows.

The shaman puts his hand on his heart.

"Adiós, amigos."

We walk over to the bikes. Climb on, rev the motors. I turn my head for a last glance at our mysterious teacher. The Rainbow Shaman has disappeared.

* * *

It's an early breakfast of egg white omelettes. Our hosts kindly give us burritos for the trip. Bernard suggests we visit the pyramids at Teotihuacan on the way to the Crystal Shaman. The GPS indicates 17 hours traveling to Teotihuacan so we decide to split the journey. Our first destination will be Golden Zone, Mazatlan, in the state of Sinaloa.

We head south on Route 15, hugging the coast, arriving comfortably by 3pm. Plenty of time to locate a hotel, drop our bags and take a walk on the beach. Surveying the stunning landscape ... toes scrunching in the soft sand ... breathing the fresh invigorating air ... admiring the beautiful turquoise water. At 5pm we amble over to the Sheik restaurant which is perched on a rocky promontory overlooking the ocean. It has exquisite furnishings, an indoor goldfish pond, and sweet piano notes wafting through the air. Our table is located on the balcony. The sunset is spectacular.

We discuss the notion of spending the next day in Mazatlan; however, we sense that something magical is calling our spirits. Stay means delay. We are eager to continue our journey. Today we travelled 7 hours, leaving a long 10-hour trip tomorrow. Naturally, we are in bed by 9pm. Sleep grabs us quickly.

Sunrise is 6.15am and heralds our departure. Southwest on Route 15D. Factoring in brief snack breaks and leg stretches, we should arrive in Teotihuacan around 5.30pm.

It's great to be on the open road. The bike-to-bike communication system is working perfectly so our lengthy silences are punctuated with gregarious chatter. We are passing the halfway mark at Guadalajara when Bernard makes a tentative enquiry.

You still interested in learning as we travel?

"A succinct lecture will keep me awake."

There will be a quiz once we reach our destination.

"Primed and listening."

Are you familiar with the term Pre-Columbian or Pre-Contact Americas?

"Remind me."

The Pre-Columbian era denotes the history of the Americas before the appearance of significant European influences. Pre-Columbian refers to the time preceding Christopher Columbus' four voyages from Spain to the Americas during 1492-1504. The alternative term Pre-Contact is also used.

"Understood."

***Mesoamerica** is a region and cultural area in the Americas, extending from central Mexico through Belize, Guatemala, Honduras, El Salvador,*

Nicaragua to the north-western border of Costa Rica, within which Pre-Contact societies flourished for about 3,000 years before the Spanish colonisation of the Americas in the 15th and 16th centuries. Historians chronicle five major civilisations: the Olmec, the Teotihuacan, the Toltec, the Mexica (Aztec), the Maya. These civilisations consolidated power (with the exception of the politically fragmented Maya) and extended their influence across Mesoamerica in the spheres of politics, trade, technology, art and theology.

"Elucidate the five major civilisations."

The **Olmec** *civilisation (1500-400 BC), located in the present-day states of Veracruz and Tabasco, introduced novel government, economics, pyramid-temples, mathematics, astronomy, writing, art and religion. Olmec is a Nahuatl word meaning 'rubber people'. The primary Olmec deity was the Feathered Serpent.*

Teotihuacan *(pronounced Teao-tea-wa-kaan) is both the name of a civilisation and its main city located in the present-day Valley of Mexico, northeast of Mexico City. After the decline of the Olmec, the Teotihuacan dominated during 200 BC - 800 AD, even influencing contemporary Maya civilisation. The city accommodates many architecturally significant Pre-Contact pyramids, including the Temple of Quetzalcoatl (aka Temple of the Feathered Serpent), the Pyramid of the Sun (third-largest pyramid in the world) and the Pyramid of the Moon. Teotihuacan is a Nahuatl word meaning 'birthplace of the gods', reflecting mysterious Nahua creation myths.*

The **Toltec** *civilisation (800-1000 AD) was a culture located in Tollan, the present-day Tula Valley, northwest of Mexico City in the state of Hidalgo. Archaeological records are vague and mystical. Tollan was ruled by Quetzalcoatl, a mysterious godlike being who was later exiled and went on to establish a new city elsewhere in Mesoamerica. Toltec is a Nahuatl word meaning 'craftsman of the highest level'. The Toltec were major traders in obsidian.*

As the Toltec civilisation declined, the Valley of Mexico became politically fragmented. A desert people called the **Mexica** *(pronounced*

Meshica) entered the arena and by 1400 AD were ruling as the head of a Triple Alliance. This alliance comprised their capital city Tenochtitlan (present-day Mexico City) and two other Mexica cities, Texcoco and Tlacopan. The Triple Alliance expanded its empire far beyond the Valley of Mexico, conquering numerous city-states throughout Mesoamerica. At its zenith, the Mexica culture was replete with complex mythological and religious traditions and extraordinary art and architecture. Tenochtitlan was possibly the largest city in the world during this period.

Located at the sacred precinct in Tenochtitlan were several venerated buildings. At the top of the Great Temple or Temple Mayor were two twin temples, one dedicated to Tlaloc, the god of rain, the other to Huitzilopochtli, the god of war. Nearby were the Pyramid of Tezcatlipoca, the Sun Temple of Tonatiuh, and the Temple of Quetzalcoatl.

The origin of the Mexica is mysterious. It is said they migrated from a place called Aztlan in the north-western deserts. (Sounds intriguingly similar to 'Atlantis'). Before they changed their name to the Mexica they were called the ***Aztec****. The language of the Aztec was Nahuatl (pronounced Nah-what). Their discovery and founding of Tenochtitlan was the fulfilment of an ancient prophecy: that the wandering tribes would create a formidable city whose location would be signalled by an eagle eating a snake while perched on top of a cactus. (An image intriguingly similar to a feathered serpent).*

The present-day designation 'Mexico' derives from their newly adopted name 'Mexica'. After the Spanish siege lead by Hernan Cortes, the Mexica (Aztec) civilisation collapsed in 1521.

The ***Maya*** *civilisation began around 2600 BC and continued until the Columbian contact in 1500 AD. The territory of the Maya covered a third of Mesoamerica, extending from the present-day Honduras, Guatemala and Belize through the south-eastern states of Mexico. The numerous Maya city-states never achieved political coherence; nonetheless, they exerted an immense intellectual influence upon the* *other major civilisations in the spheres of mathematics, astronomy, calendars, architecture, art and writing. Mayan hieroglyphic script was the only fully developed writing system of Pre-Contact Americas; mostly inscribed on stone, pottery, wood or perishable books made from bark paper. The sacred books of the Maya were burned in 1562.*

Palenque was an extensive Pre-Contact Maya city located in the present-day Chiapas State. Its stone temples are renowned for architectural sophistication and fine sculptures; the ruins are immersed in a jungle of cedar, mahogany and sapodilla trees. Significant structures at Palenque include: Temple of the Inscriptions, Temple of the Sun, Temple of the Count, Temple of the Cross and Temple of the Foliated Cross.

Chichen Itza was a large Pre-Contact Maya city located in the present-day Yucatan State. It is now a UNESCO World Heritage Site. Well known stone monuments at this site include El Castillo (aka Temple of Kukulcan, which roughly translates as 'feathered serpent'), the Temple of Warriors and the Great Ball Court.

"That's interesting. Every major civilisation revered the Feathered Serpent. Do you have more information?"

***Quetzalcoatl** (pronounced Ketzal-quat) was one of the most important gods in Mesoamerica. He was originally known as the Feathered Serpent or Plumed Serpent because he appeared as a snake with feathers or wings. The name Quetzalcoatl comes from the Nahuatl words quetzal meaning 'emerald plumed bird' and coatl meaning 'serpent'. The worship of a feathered serpent began with the Olmec and veneration of the deity appears to have spread throughout Mesoamerica up until 1519 AD. Quetzalcoatl occupied a central place in the pantheon of the Mexica (Aztec) people. The Maya used the names Kukulcan and Gukumatz which roughly translate as 'feathered serpent'. The true nature of Quetzalcoatl is shrouded in myth and mystery.*

"Hmm. Perplexing and intriguing."

Lecture complete.

"Thanks, bro."

I open the throttle and we race down the highway. Exhilaration surges through my veins. Bernard's jubilant *Whoo hoos!* suffuse the blurring landscape. Time seems to disappear.

We arrive in Teotihuacan at 6pm. It is easy to find a decent hotel. Soon we are checked in and alleviating our fatigue with cold drinks in the lounge. It's been a long trip and we are looking forward to a hearty dinner and restful sleep.

* * *

The secret to pleasant sightseeing is preparation and an early start. Firstly, you need to check the weather conditions. Will you need a sun hat or rain jacket or extra layers of clothing? Secondly, always carry at least one bottle of water. I prefer a compact, lightweight backpack with a compartment containing a reservoir of water and easy-access drinking tube. Thirdly, you need to check the opening and closing times. Most tourists wake late and visit sites from 10am. To avoid the crowds and midday sun it is essential to arrive early.

Teotihuacan opens at 7am. We cruise through Gate 3 and park our bikes near the Pyramid of the Moon. In Mexico City the altitude is 2,240 metres above sea level. In Teotihuacan it is 2,281 metres. We have been living in Oregon and San Francisco where the altitude is negligible, hence we opt for a leisurely acclimatising pace.

We slowly climb the stone steps of the Pyramid of the Moon. The sun is peeking gently over the nearby mountain, illuminating a cloudless sky. Beautiful start to the day. From the top of the pyramid we gaze south along the Avenue of the Dead (*Calzada de los Muertos*). Further down the avenue on the left is the Pyramid of the Sun. At the end of the avenue is the Citadel (*La Ciudadela*). It is a magnificent vista. Deserves the name 'birthplace of the gods'.

We descend then amble toward the Pyramid of the Sun. According to the pamphlet it is 71 metres high with 248 steps. I groan quietly, sip some water, begin the ascent. The spectacular view is worth it. This UNESCO World Heritage Site comprises dozens of smaller temples, palaces and residential compounds. You could spend hours exploring it all. The pamphlet also mentions that the Pyramid of the Sun was built over a natural cave. Mesoamericans believed that caves were gateways to the spiritual world.

Afterward we make our way to the Citadel. This vast arena was home to the ancient city's administration. It also contains the fascinating Temple of Quetzalcoatl. I am standing before the temple … enthralled by the sculptures and engravings of feathered serpents … the hairs on my arms are bristling … a strange energy is rippling through me … sensations beyond my comprehension … leaving me confounded and bemused.

Finally we visit the Museum of the Site of Teotihuacan (*Museo de Sitio*) located near the Pyramid of the Sun, which displays fabulous artefacts, sculptures, pottery, obsidian, and a miniature version of the entire city.

There are plenty of local restaurants so we hop on our bikes and find a nice place for lunch. Bernard's countenance reflects contentment. My energy is an amalgam of satisfaction and apprehension. I am trying not to think about our next destination.

* * *

My sleep was restless. We are venturing into unknown territory. The words of the Rainbow Shaman haunt me. 'Once you open that door, your sword and shield consist of impeccability, altruism and radical respect.' That I can do. 'The secret is to align yourself with the beings of light that exist in the multi-dimensions.' How is that accomplished?

Bernard appears unusually tired this morning. He shuffles around the bedroom, then steps into the shower. Hopefully that will give him a boost. Once he is done, I have a quick wash and we trudge to breakfast.

Man, I am wiped today.

"It's not like you."

Something drained my energy.

"Anything I can do?"

Let me have a cup of coffee.

"No, dude. Not happening."

He sighs deeply. Hands on temples.

"We must follow the rules."

A weird presence. Can't explain it.

Alex, something's gripping me. Like tentacles.

Out of my depth. Try to hide my fear.

"You mean negative thoughts?"

My words sound pathetic.

It's eating my energy.

He seems helpless. Darkness seeping. Suddenly I feel compassion melding with anger. I will not allow this! My gaze defocuses. I am back at the Temple of Quetzalcoatl ... hairs on my arms bristling ... sensing the powerful light inside me ... energy surging ... extend my palm toward Bernard ... hear my mouth strongly command "No!" ... darkness recoils ... "Return to your origin" ... whirling ... diminishing ... disappears.

Bernard shakes his head.

Wow. What did you do?

Shrug my shoulders.

It's gone. I feel normal again.

Relieved countenance.

Where did you learn sorcery?

"No idea what's occurring."

You are connected to Quetzalcoatl.

"What made you say that?"

The words tumbled out my mouth.

"Maybe I am aligned with a being of light."

His eyes are twinkling.

Ultra-cool.

Laughter tickles me.

"What's happening to us?"

Don't know. But I like it.

"You nervous to meet the Crystal Shaman?"

Why be nervous? He serves the Light.

"When I grow up, I want to be you."

A smile dashes across his face.

We have to heal our pain and fear.

"Where did I hear that?"

The Rainbow Shaman.

"Oh yeah."

Stroke my beard thoughtfully.

"You think the shamans are related?"

They both have sobriquets.

"Sobri-whats?"

Code names, nick names, aliases.

"Maybe they're from another planet."

A peculiar shiver rushes through me.

Bernard suddenly appears serious.

How far away is the Crystal Shaman?

I consult the GPS.

"The town of Eloxochitlan de Flores Magon is 5 hours from here."

Shall we leave after breakfast?

Observing his shifting demeanour. What's with him?

"Sure. Just check out and depart."

Forty minutes later we are on the road.

Bernard is quiet and sombre. It gives me time to reflect on my situation. A lot has happened since I left Oregon. Was that only ten days ago? Feels like a different life. I don't ascribe to the New Age notion of previous lives; it's more like a book with many chapters. Childhood, adolescence, first love, heartbreak, career, marriage, divorce, recent work, travelling, shamanism. They're all chapters, all previous lives. Perhaps my soul is writing a book of adventures.

The motto '**experience before ideology**' is very appealing. Have to admit I don't have many beliefs. I am jaded and confused. However, rooting myself in atheism, agnosticism, solipsism or nihilism is just as limiting and futile as rooting myself in religion, spiritualism or superstition. It makes more sense to loosen my grip on concepts and beliefs and open myself to the flow of life and direct experience.

I have discovered an underlying fear in me. Introspection tells me it was always here. Well, at least from early childhood. Has it affected my relationships? My career choices? Have my rigid boundaries impeded the river of life? Fear indicates previous wounds or traumas. Unresolved issues that need processing.

What did the Rainbow Shaman say? 'You now require slower journeys, deep healing and lesson learning.' Subdued sigh. Yeah, I agree.

We arrive in Eloxochitlan de Flores Magon at 1pm. Tummies are rumbling so we search for a suitable place to eat. Bernard explains that 96% of the town's residents speak the indigenous Mazatec language. Unfortunately our Spanish is poor and Mazatec non-existent.

There are 320 million people in the USA of which 41 million are native Spanish speakers. That's 13% of the population, a figure predicted to increase every year. The highest concentrations of native Spanish speakers are in New Mexico (47%), California and Texas (both 38%) and Arizona (30%). I really ought to learn the language.

The verdant scenery is breathtaking. Trees blanket the Sierra Mazateca. The highest peak is 2,600 metres; we are situated at a comfortable 1,400 metres. Mist hangs in the distant valley. The weather is 25 degrees Celsius with clear blue sky. Warm sun soaking into my skin. Chorus of bird calls caressing my ears.

Bernard is smiling happily.

This is great, man. Love it.

"Yeah. It feels good."

Where do we go from here?

"You asking me?"

A stray dog limps toward us. Meek and friendly. Tail wagging. We feed him the scraps from our table. I cautiously inspect his paw. Gingerly extract a tiny barb. Stroke his head. He looks me deep in the eyes, as if searching my soul. Then he barks loudly and runs away.

Laughter grips then overwhelms me.

Bernard stares at me inquisitively.

What's with you, dude?

Takes a while to recover.

Stranger approaching. Mazatec. Slightly built. Long grey hair. Worn out clothes. Eyes the colour of the sky. Probably in his seventies. Gnarled walking stick assisting his unsteady gait.

"You the man who helped my dog?"

I nod tentatively.

"Why?"

Bernard quickly interjects.

We mean no harm, sir.

Piercing gaze falls upon my friend.

"Why?"

All beings deserve compassion and kindness.

The stick whirls swiftly, the end landing on Bernard's shoulder. Is the old man demented? My companion could flatten him in a heartbeat.

Impeccability, altruism, radical respect.

Smile crinkles his face.

"Welcome to my world. You will be staying with me. Duties include shopping, cooking and cleaning. You will be my apprentices."

Yes sir.

I nod solemnly.

"Fetch your bikes. Follow me."

Meander slowly after the master.

I glance across at Bernard and grin.

The Crystal Shaman has been stalking us.

* * *

It's a humble two-bedroom property. Immersed in a forest of oak and pine. Spectacular unbroken views. Birds chirping cheerfully in the trees. Eerie atmosphere. The shaman no doubt has a reputation, which ensures he has no neighbours.

He seems prepared for visitors. Our room has separate beds with individual wardrobes. There is a communal shower and toilet. Comfortable lounge. Kitchen with small dining area. The house is clean and tidy.

The shaman lays out the terms and conditions. A very reasonable weekly fee covers accommodation and services. In addition, he outlines the residential duties. We graciously agree. Bernard and I quietly negotiate. Turns out he enjoys cooking; cleaning will be my responsibility. We can do grocery shopping together. Everything is settled.

The Crystal Shaman beckons us to walk with him. We sit under a resplendent sweet gum tree. Sunlight glimmers upon the flaming red and orange leaves.

The stare is resolute and unwavering.

"Are you ready for these journeys?"

Absolutely, sir.

I assent softly.

"Most consciousness is not ready for what I know. Patience and empathy are the most important attributes for me. I wait for your boundaries to drop and minds to awaken. I watch you wrestle with your ideologies and stories. I quietly smile as you take detours. Detours are uncomfortable but facilitate great learning. We all get there in the end. These journeys involve healing and transcendence. Energy exchange. Shifting the resonance of consciousness."

Bernard is enthralled.

The shaman gestures toward the sky.

A Red-tailed Hawk swoops silently past us.

Ambience transforms to other-worldly.

Crystal Shaman is radiating ethereal starlight.

Explains how he acquired his sobriquet.

The forest becomes completely silent.

Inscrutable gaze unravels our souls.

A sacrosanct whisper.

"What if everything you believe about yourself is not true? What if your convictions about life are challenged and start to crumble?

What if on the other side of your ideologies exists deep, abiding happiness? What if you forgot your origin and the only way Home is to locate the fractal keys?"

He suddenly stands up, ambles through the trees, and disappears.

Inexplicably, we know he will not return tonight.

We saunter to the house. Alone for the evening.

Crystal Shaman has left us much to ponder.

* * *

The master appears at the door early the next morning. Bernard and I have been up for a while, probably the result of excitement and apprehension. We have already showered and eaten breakfast.

We are summoned to the vibrant sweet gum tree. There is no San Marcos blanket; instead we repose on a pile of crackling amber leaves. It's another warm and sunny day. The forest is ablaze with colour and song. Stunning location for mystical lectures.

He smiles briefly.

"You both bear the mark of a shaman. Hence, you are my apprentices. This carries a great responsibility. Listen carefully and absorb the teachings."

Understood.

I nod devoutly.

"**You are consciousness. You are a transmitter and receiver of consciousness.** You are swimming in a sea of consciousness. Your beliefs, stories and ideologies restrict your transceiver. You absorb the consciousness of limited humans and dwell in a consensual reality. Earth reality is created by all of you. Together you are manifesting and immersing in one television channel. As if this is the only reality. Meanwhile you are missing out on thousands of other channels. And the potential to create a beautiful world.

"**Entheogens retune your transceiver**, first temporarily then permanently. They break open the restricting barriers and perspectives and show you the other television channels. As always, this is moderated by your readiness and resistance. Entheogens merely extend an invitation. Sometimes your beliefs and fears get in the way and you refuse to watch a particular channel. When that happens, the higher beings disengage and patiently wait.

"You are in charge of your own evolution. If you turn a fractal key and open a cosmic door, it is up to you to walk through it. You have free will. You decide your perspective. When you encounter foreign concepts, you have a choice: surrender and learn, or resist and stay. Consequently, evolution can be a very long process. A relentless journey. You call these lifetimes.

"When an entheogen temporarily retunes your awareness, capitalise on the opportunity. Open your mind to the novel concepts unfolding before you, the strangeness of other worlds, the teachings of the beings of light. Many humans have a critically restricted consciousness – unable to accept differences in race, culture, ethnicity, gender, sexual orientation. Imagine the struggle when they encounter exotic beings in higher dimensions. You need to accept All That Is. Your attitudes and choices determine your progress on the Path.

"From one perspective, the universe is an interconnected network of consciousness, every being linked to every other being. From another perspective, the universe consists of layers of consciousness or multi-dimensions. From a higher vantage point, you understand the universe as rays of the Sun or emanations of God or radiances of the Source. Ultimately, however, you will discover there is only one Consciousness. You are that one Consciousness. Entheogen journeys allow you to meet higher beings, surf the multi-dimensions, travel along the rays of light, embrace the one Consciousness and return Home."

His brow furrows sternly.

"It's time to let go your limited perspectives, adolescent attitudes and infantile ideologies. It's time to release your pain, trauma and shadows. No more fight or flight; it's time to deal. It's time to do the work. Only then will you arrive at the first rung of the Sacred Ladder."

Scratching my beard thoughtfully. Esoteric lesson.

The shaman stands to his feet and indicates a dirt path.

"Ramble down to the valley. Do not speak until you have spotted a Brown-backed Solitaire. Make sure you take sufficient water and food."

We obey the brusque instruction. Ten minutes later we are descending the slope. Silence compels us to contemplate the teachings.

The lower altitude is lush and tropical. We stroll among coffee, banana and avocado trees, Monstera vines with huge deep-fingered leaves, and chicozapote and mamey trees, which produce deliciously sweet fruit. Ravishing red-flowered mimosas are swamped by sumptuous hummingbirds. Our ramble becomes a serene and delightful meditation.

Bernard points to a nearby branch. At last we have detected a Brown-backed Solitaire. It's a greyish bird with white eye-rings and brown flight feathers. Assignment complete.

"Nice job, man."

Thanks. How's your day going?

"Alright. Digesting the concepts."

A whole other level of knowledge.

"That's for sure."

Ready to head back?

"Yeah. Let's do it."

It takes us a couple of hours.

The forest is quiet … ruffle of a gentle breeze … occasional twirling leaf … crackle of pine needles underfoot … refreshing … peaceful.

We enter the house. Drop the backpack.

Bernard decides to take a shower.

I gaze out the windows.

Nothing happening.

Wait a few minutes.

He emerges.

Seems we are alone again.

"May as well go grocery shopping."

Yeah. Fulfil our duties.

We hop on our bikes. Rev the engines.

I survey the surrounding landscape.

Where is that mysterious shaman?

* * *

I am beginning to wonder if our teacher is living here. Perhaps this house is for guests only. After breakfast we take a walk through the beautiful woods. Crisp air and warbling birdsong make for a fabulous start to the day.

A loud whistle pierces the air.

Grey-haired figure waving at us.

We stroll toward the sweet gum tree.

"Did you bring your note book?"

He taps his head furtively.

Yes sir. Open mind. Ready to absorb.

I bow courteously and sit down.

The shaman clasps his palms together.

"**Entheogen journeys** have **four crucial components**: set, setting, sitter and catalyst.

"**Set** refers to the mindset, attitude, intentions and readiness of the psychonaut. You should only journey if you are in a positive state of mind. That does not mean you have no wounds, issues or traumas. It does not mean you have no sadness, pain or fear. It means that you approach the journey with clear, positive intentions and a sense of optimism. Your mindset, attitude, intentions and readiness will influence the direction of the journey. You need to be welcoming of novel experiences. You need to be ready to face buried traumas and shadows. You need to be open to teachings that challenge your beliefs, stories and ideologies. You need to remember your navigation tools: witness, breathe, surrender. Finally, you must be willing to ask for assistance if necessary.

"**Setting** refers to the physical and psychological environment of the psychonaut. You should only embark on a journey when settled in a place that feels secure and sacred. You will be in an intensely vulnerable position so you must ensure your needs will be met. Are you at home or in a foreign environment? Are you with friends or strangers? Does the atmosphere feel supportive and loving? Are you comfortable journeying with fellow psychonauts or would you prefer a private journey which typically allows more freedom and devoted attention?

"**Sitter** refers to the shaman or trip-sitter. This is the person responsible for your well-being, the person who watches over you during your journey. Questions you need to ask: Does the sitter have experience with psychedelic journeys and with the entheogen you are going to ingest? Has the sitter discussed your state of physical and psychological health? Do you completely trust the sitter? Are you able to surrender and be vulnerable with the sitter? Does the sitter operate with impeccability, altruism and radical respect? Always journey with a shaman or sitter. Never journey alone.

"**Catalyst** refers to the psychedelic or entheogen you are going to ingest. Is this the right catalyst for your particular needs and goals? Have your physical and psychological states been calibrated to establish the ideal dosage?

"An experienced sitter always issues the following **caveat** and **warning**: You should not embark on a psychedelic journey if you are pregnant or if you have a bleeding colon or if you have a heart condition or if you have high blood pressure or if you have type 1 or type 2 diabetes or if you are prone to epilepsy or seizures or asthma or if you are under the influence of drugs including marijuana or if you are under the influence of medication including antibiotics and antidepressants and antihistamines or if you are experiencing severe mental or physical health challenges for example schizophrenia or bipolar disorder.

"The sitter also issues the following **pre-emptive instruction**: At least one week prior to and one week following and during your psychedelic journey you should abstain from all non-prescription medicines and recreational drugs and alcohol and caffeine and sexual activity."

He earnestly scrutinises our faces.

"Anything you want to ask? Anything you need to declare?"

I shuffle uncomfortably. Shake my head.

We meet all the requirements, sir.

My eyelids flutter. I stifle a yawn.

The shaman slaps the ground with his stick.

"Pay close attention."

Startled, I perk up.

"**Entheogen journeys** are characterised by **five stages**. You may experience one, a few or all of these stages during a particular journey.

"**Physical**. The first stage of a psychedelic journey involves physical and sensory changes. Being forewarned will help you relax and settle into the experience. Physical changes may include increased heart rate, blurred vision, twitches, mild tremors, sweating, feeling cold, blue hands and feet, nausea, upset tummy. Sensory changes may include heightened sensitivity to light and sound, perceptual distortions and entoptic phenomena (visual images occurring inside the eye). Fractal patterns often occur during this stage.

"**Psychodynamic**. This is usually the second stage of a psychedelic journey; however, you sometimes jump ahead to other stages. In the psychodynamic stage unconscious material surfaces into the conscious mind. This may include repressed emotions and memories; buried traumas; ingrained patterns, attitudes and beliefs; and hidden aspects of your personality. You may experience a range of frightening and beautiful visions. This is your opportunity to witness, accept and embrace your shadows.

"**Perinatal**. When most of your unconscious issues are resolved, you may regress and re-experience aspects of life in the womb or your birth. If your birth was traumatic you may experience a catharsis.

"**Past Lives**. This advanced stage may reveal past life memories, traumas, karma, lessons and life scripts. You may hear a voice or sense the presence of a guide. You are often invited to make reparations and changes.

"**Transcendent**. This is the highest stage. You usually enter this stage after numerous psychedelic journeys; however, you may move through all stages or leap to this stage in a single psychedelic journey. Experiences may include loss of personal identity, meeting higher beings, accessing the multi-dimensions, assimilation of sacred teachings, dying to self, spiritual rebirth, immersing into the Source or Light. Depending on your readiness and resistance, you may shift between ecstasy and fear."

Bernard is rubbing his chin.

Wow. That is interesting.

I nod ebulliently.

"Know what to expect."

A navigation map.

"Exactly."

The shaman is staring at us intently.

Grips his walking stick. Stands to his feet.

"Enough for today. Tomorrow you journey."

His hand flourishes affably toward the trees.

"Go and play. See you in the morning."

Questions are clearly not welcome.

I look at Bernard and shrug.

We spend the afternoon throwing a flying disc to each other, exploring the lush terrain and observing wildlife. It is good to be away from newspapers, radio, television and the stresses of ordinary existence. Our bodies are recalling primal instincts, our minds resetting to the tranquillity of nature. Probably an astute way to prepare us for journeys.

Bernard cooks a delicious dinner. I clean the kitchen.

The shaman is nowhere to be found.

Nothing to do but be.

It's an early night.

Sleep enfolds us.

* * *

I am on fire this morning. Tempted to go for a long run in the forest. Bernard declines my invitation. Not his style. Slip on my trainers. Warm up, stretch. Deep breaths. Fresh invigorating air. Soft earth comfortably supporting my knees. Birdsong filling the empty spaces. Exhilarating.

Fifteen minutes in, come to a clearing. Hazy light shimmering through the treetops. Hairs on my arms suddenly bristling. Weird sensations. Crackle of twigs. Stand still. Wait.

Few metres ahead. Wolf staring at me. Grey with light brown fur.

Transfixed by commanding yet familiar energy.

Pads toward me. Long legs and sleek body.

Tilts it head. Primal inspection.

Eyes the colour of the sky.

Ambience is unruffled.

Turns away.

Urge to follow.

Picks up speed.

Running through the forest alongside a wolf. Utterly bizarre. Feels so natural.

Bernard is going to think I am crazy.

Lost in the moment. Time disappears.

Merging. Nature is in me.

Oh, there is the house.

Alone again.

Hands on knees, catch my breath.

My young friend ambles over.

Hey dude. Good run?

"Yeah. Tired now."

You were gone an hour.

"Seriously?"

Uh huh.

"Carried away."

Ready for breakfast?

"Granola?"

Hot breakfast.

"Nice."

Sustenance for our journeys.

"Good plan."

I jump in the shower; get dressed.

An hour later our illustrious shaman arrives.

Smile creases his face.

"You boys ready?"

Bernard gives a friendly salute.

I nod enthusiastically.

"Come with me."

We stroll for ten minutes. He halts beside a woody-stemmed climbing vine with white flowers.

"Let me introduce you to **Ololiuqui** (*pronounced Oh-loh-lee-oo-kee*). This vine (*Turbina corymbosa* aka *Rivea corymbosa*) belongs to the Morning Glory family."

He breaks open one of the small fleshy fruits and extracts the single seed.

"Ololiuqui is a Nahuatl word meaning 'round thing', referring to the spherical seeds of this plant. We use these seeds for medicinal and entheogenic purposes. For sacred journeys the seeds are ground and placed in a cup of water for infusion. The seeds are then strained and the psychonaut drinks the brew. Onset occurs after 45 minutes and effects last 4-6 hours."

What's the active ingredient?

"Interesting question. Laboratory analysis has revealed that Ololiuqui seeds contain **LSA** (**lysergic acid amide**) which essentially means that our sacred seeds are a natural form of LSD (lysergic acid diethylamide). Ololiuqui has been used for thousands of years in Mesoamerican civilisations. It was certainly in the diverse pharmacopoeia of the Maya and Mexica (Aztec)."

Awesome! Ancient entheogens.

"Secrets are being revealed."

Unveiling of the esoteric path.

"Let's return to the house."

He leads us into the spacious lounge.

Butterflies are flitting in my tummy.

The gnarled stick taps the wooden floor.

"Listen carefully, my protégés.

"Before commencing an entheogen journey always **clear your chakras and energy field** then **seal them in Light**. You also need to clear the energy of the journey venue and seal it in Light. Once that is complete you invite the presence of the beings of light."

Why do we clear energy?

"The human energy field tends to collect negative energy from interacting in a low-resonance world. Negative or dark energy will impede your journey. You clear the venue and create a sacred space for two reasons: (a) to ensure protection (b) to encourage the presence of the beings of light."

How do we clear energy?

"There are many energy techniques that can be used, including Reiki, burning Palo Santo, or smudging with Sage and Cedar. If your sitter is a shaman then you can surrender to their expertise. However, you need to learn to clear the energy."

Will you teach us?

"Rituals and incantations?"

Bernard glances at me.

I solemnly interject.

"The real deal."

The shaman tilts his head and winks at me.

"Sure, El lobo."

El lobo? That means 'the wolf'.

What's going on here?

He claps his hands loudly.

"Here is the rule:

"**Faith guides intention. Intention guides energy.**

"Less evolved beings put their faith in intermediate devices like rattles, feathers, incense and herbs. Those devices work because faith guides intention. Advanced beings use faith directly."

How do you mean?

"Bernard, clear Alex's energy."

My friend shuffles uncomfortably.

"Do not move. Speak if you must. Otherwise simply command with your thoughts."

Uh … I invoke that all negative and dark energy leave Alex's chakras and energy field.

"Where are you sending it?"

I don't know.

"Return to your origin."

Aha.

Deep breath.

I invoke that all negative and dark energy leave Alex's chakras and energy field. Return to your origin.

"Don't say. Command. Have faith!"

I invoke that all negative and dark energy leave Alex's chakras and energy field. Return to your origin!

"Now sense Alex's energy. Notice the shift?"

Yes, I do.

"Utilise strong thoughts until his energy is clear."

Bernard closes his eyes tightly. Head bobbing.

Strange. I feel lighter, more relaxed.

I believe it is complete.

"Now seal in Light."

Tell me how.

"Invoke that the Source or the Light or the highest divinity flows around Alex and cocoons him. Command that he will be protected during his journey."

Head bobbing again.

"Well done, Bernard."

The shaman waves his hand over him.

"I hereby clear and seal your energy too."

Wow. In just two seconds.

Gazes earnestly at me. "What's next?"

Let me think. Oh yes, clear the venue. Scrunch my eyes. Shout in my mind. Command. Invoke that all dark and negative energy leave the venue. Return to origin. Wait and sense. Couple more times. Hmm. Feels emptier. Invoke that the room is sealed in Light. Yes, that's it.

"Impressive, El lobo."

I grin with satisfaction.

"The secret, my protégés, is to keep the power within you. No need for external tools and devices. Be real. Be free."

Where have I heard that before?

"Bernard, would you like to do the honours?"

Invite the beings of light?

"Of course."

Beings of light from the multi-dimensions, be here now.

"The tone required is sacredness and respect."

Hairs on my arms bristling. Ambience dramatically shifting.

Can the shaman see the beings? Or just sense them like me?

Arcane laughter.

"You'll see them soon, Alex."

Out of my depth. Not going to ask.

The cryptic shaman heaves a sigh.

"You mostly **journey in darkness and silence**. Occasionally you will journey in daylight in nature. For a specific therapeutic purpose, music is sometimes used. Amazonian shamans often sing *icaros* during journeys to protect and shift energy. However, your journeys with me will be in silence. Questions and requests are always welcome."

He draws the curtains, then gives us each an eyemask, box of tissues and two bottles of water. Points to the sofas.

"Make yourselves comfortable. There are plenty of extra blankets in case of temperature fluctuations."

Bernard raises his hand.

Why are we journeying during the day?

"Night journeys tend to conflict with biorhythms. It is hard to process issues or travel the multi-dimensions when your body is trying to fall asleep. We want to minimise or eliminate physical stress. The journeys should focus purely on the psychological and spiritual."

Some people say suffering is necessary.

"Unfortunately many shamans have been tainted by religion, particularly Catholicism. The ideology of purging and suffering infiltrates their practices. What benefits come from physical discomfort and distress?"

Is any touching allowed?

"Hugs and hand-holding. As much as you request."

Are you going to blow tobacco smoke on us?

"You want to inhale toxic vapours? Nicotine is a poison. It serves no spiritual purpose. You will not be snorting tobacco or inhaling tobacco smoke."

Should we hold intentions?

"Once you have ingested the entheogen, you will sit quietly and reflect on your intentions. You can also inform the beings of light. Remember, having particular intentions does not guarantee the content or outcome of your journey. Heed the shamanic adage: You don't always have the journey you want; instead, you seem to have the journey you need."

Any final advice?

"Enter your journey with courage and humility. Wounds, issues and shadows will surface. Expect insights and teachings to accompany that uncomfortable process. If you encounter something that causes fear in you, do not fight or flight. That will make your journey very challenging. If you feel unable to engage with an event or being, simply revert to your navigation tools: witness, breathe, surrender. When you have sufficient courage, leap into whatever you are facing, walk through the door, flow into the vortex, engage with the beings, embrace the strange and novel reality.

"Everything is happening here now during your journey so you can travel to any person or life event where reparation needs to be made, to apologise, forgive, retrieve power or expunge karma. Forgiving yourself is especially powerful and liberating."

The Crystal Shaman hands us each a small glass.

"Drink when you are ready."

Neither of us hesitate.

"Be still. Focus on your intentions."

Check water is within reach. Eyemasks on. Try to relax.

It's weird laying here waiting for an unknown substance to take effect. I have no idea what to expect. Psychonauts are pioneers of their own minds. Adventurers within their own souls. Anything can happen.

Been about 40 minutes. Mouth slightly dry. Feel spaced out. Tingling in my hands. Getting a bit cold. Request another blanket. Shivering. Flashes of colour. Wow. My voice sounds distant. Okay, these body changes are normal. Acceptance. I am safe.

There is that sexy woman from the television show. Curves. Finger beckoning me. 'Come closer. Give yourself to me. It's alright. Sexuality is part of love. Surrender. Let go.' Whoa. Feel her passionate kisses. Aroused. Bright red swirling tunnel.

Walking behind her. 'You must love all parts of me. I am a mother too. Let me nurture you.' Panic. Don't want to be smothered. Blackness. Anger. Fear. Oh my God. Wait. Breathe. Yes, breathe. 'I love you, Alex.' Is that me screaming?

Darkness. Lost. Can't find my way. In the woods. At night. Something out there. Rustle of leaves draws my attention. Huge psychedelic snake coiled in a tree. 'Waiting for you. Waiting for you.' Why is everything so frightening? Witness. Wait. Am I facing myself? Are these my issues? Oh yeah … fear. 'Are you ready, my child?' Don't fight, don't flight. Oh my God. Help me!

Grey wolf in the distance. Alpha male. Move toward it. Long legs and sleek body. Grey paws. Rhythmic breathing. I am a wolf. We run together for a while. 'You are not alone, El lobo.' Familiar yaps and howls. More wolves. We are a pack! I belong to a pack! Alpha consoling me. 'Settle down. Get used to the terrain. Learn to navigate it. We will protect you.'

Light of dawn suffusing the forest. Piercing whistle in the sky. Outstretched wings of a Golden Eagle. Contented. Free. Alone. Raise my head, yelling at it. "You are meant to be with your partner! Why are you flying alone?" Recognition. It's Bernard. Love that guy.

Suddenly feel exhausted. Been running for ages. Locate a mound of leaves. Need to rest. Eyes heavy. My pack is near. Lay my head on soft fur. Let go. Drift away.

I awake to hazy light. Where am I? Oh, the sofa. Faint smile of the shaman. Bottle of water in my hand. Can't speak. Drink. Close my eyes again. Sleep.

Wake much later. Hungry. Offered a sandwich. Slurred thank you. Guided into my bed. Soft pillow. Warm blankets. Ah, bliss.

* * *

Stumble into the shower. Hot water will shake my grogginess. Dry off. Get dressed. Check the clock: 10am. Wha-a-a-t? How is that possible?

Note on the kitchen table: 'Integrate your journeys. See you tomorrow. CS.'

Alrighty then. Guess we are alone again.

Eat some granola then trudge outside.

Bernard is sitting beneath the sweet gum tree.

Not sure if he is meditating so tread quietly.

His eyes immediately open.

Morning dude. You're alive!

"Mind if I sit with you?"

Sure. Be my guest.

I drop onto the soft leaves.

"That was an intense journey."

Yeah. You screamed at one point.

"Hope I didn't disturb you."

No. It actually helped me. I was struggling. Wrestling with the experience. Concerned about my body. When you screamed I realised it was hard for both of us. Ololiuqui is not a brief in-and-out journey.

"Once you ingest, you are committed."

You have to adapt to each new entheogen.

"I was told to learn to navigate the terrain."

It is dissimilar to 5-MeO. Threw me off my game.

"Exactly. New terrain. Different navigation."

I eventually surrendered. But it took me a while.

"What happened on your journey?"

Heard beings talking to me. Encouraging me to let go. Later they were chatting among themselves saying I was not ready. They kept changing tactics … kindness, cajoling, mocking … opening different scenes … then they disappeared into the background. After you screamed, I decided to risk it all. Suddenly I was in a forest. My wing was limp. Hopping on the ground. Took ages to stretch my wing. It slowly healed in the morning sun.

"Wait a minute. A wing?"

I was a Golden Eagle. Same consciousness, different body. Finally took flight. Awesome. At one point, I looked down and saw a grey wolf. Felt drawn to the animal but remained hovering above the treetops.

"No way!"

What is it?

"I became a grey wolf and saw you flying in the sky. I saw you."

Bernard is staring at me curiously.

Alex, I became an eagle. There was no reality except what I was inhabiting. Are you saying we shared a reality?

"I transformed into a wolf, running with my pack. Did we go into the forest last night? Or was it a shared hallucination?"

That was no hallucination, dude. I went somewhere. Either this forest or another dimension.

"Wow. What if everything the shamans are teaching us is true?"

My friend bursts into laughter.

I am stunned. Are we really just a point of consciousness? Travelling along a ray of light? Our position dictating our perspective dictating our reality? What is reality?

It's a whole new world, Alex. Open your eyes.

No wonder we need an integration day.

I stand up. Stretch my body.

"Going for a walk. Need to ponder and digest."

No worries. It's why I was meditating.

"See you later, brother."

His eyes flutter closed.

I spend the rest of the day in nature. Trying to absorb and understand the experiences.

Seems the strategy works for both of us. In the evening we settle and enjoy a delicious dinner. The atmosphere feels peaceful. Tomorrow is another day. Perhaps we will have more answers.

* * *

The Crystal Shaman arrives at 11am. Long grey hair frames a serious countenance.

"Time to roll up the sleeves and do some work. No coasting today."

Sounds ominous. Probably referring to our last journeys.

We take our positions on the sofas.

Bernard, as always, has questions.

Where did we go yesterday?

Inscrutable smile.

"You have your eye so tightly pressed to the keyhole that you have forgotten the keyhole exists. On which side of the door are you standing? What if you exist simultaneously in many dimensions? What would happen if you awoke and discovered that truth? How would your life be?"

My friend looks astonished.

"The question is: Who are you?"

Silence descends.

Inner struggle. Turmoil.

"Who are you? What are you? What does that mean when 'I' is an illusion that you are creating? You don't exist. You are nothing but the flow of Life expressing itself in multiple radiances. You are pure consciousness swimming in Consciousness."

Wow. Lost me at 'illusion'.

Penetrating gaze turns toward me.

"Who are you, Alex? Human, wolf, engineer, lover?"

Racking my brains. Are those just roles I play?

Pure awareness. Pure consciousness.

The shaman applauds jubilantly.

"Nothing more. Nothing less."

It is quiet for a long while.

Did our last journeys leave unfinished business?

"Of course. When you do consecutive entheogen journeys (with at least a day between for rest and integration) you will notice the next journey often commences where the last one ended, especially if a particular issue is not resolved. You tend to revisit issues and teachings until you make the necessary internal changes (adopting new thoughts, feelings, beliefs) and sometimes external changes (shifting relationships, work, abode)."

Bernard ponders the ceiling.

Witness, breathe, surrender.

Glances at the shaman.

Ok, I'm ready.

I have butterflies before every journey. Adventuring into the unknown. Hope I can adroitly navigate the terrain this time. Nod my head in assent.

We drink the Ololiuqui infusion.

Eyemask on. Clear and seal my energy.

Hmm ... intention ... delve into and process my fear.

Waiting for onset. Body tremoring. Nausea. Is that nerves? Ignore physical symptoms; a natural side effect of ingesting an entheogen.

Enormous screech in my head. Black swirling vortex. 'I am coming for you. Going to destroy you. Your life is not your own. I hate you. I hate you!' Clawed hands. Ferocious energy. Dangerous eyes. Out of control. "No, don't hurt me!" My voice is shouting. Oh my God. I know those eyes. Fear engulfs me. Falling into quicksand. Struggling to move. It's my mother. Unpredictable. Love. Anger. Smothering. Distant. Overwhelming. Unavailable. Euphoric. Depressed. Suicidal. Silent. Screaming. Absent. No matter what I say or do. Helpless.

Twilight forest. Dark being chasing me. I see the wolves. Bound toward my pack. Alpha snarls at me. 'Stop running. Turn and face the tormentor.' Mouth is dry. Ears pinned back. Circling the dark figure. Unison of howls behind me. The fur along my spine is bristling ... head lowers ... reveal my teeth. Howls getting louder. Sweat pours from me. Nausea flip flops my tummy.

Launch my attack. "No more! It's enough!" Jaw aches. Face on fire. Flurry of madness. Intense pain. "Aaargghh!" Sudden *whoosh!* Sinister entity dissipates. "Oh my God. Oh my God! Oh my God!" Tears burning my cheeks. Sobbing. Relief. Freedom.

Open my eyes. Shaman handing me a tissue. Blow my nose. Crying. Smiling. Reach for my water. Another tissue. Blow. Eyes flicker closed. Giggles tickling my tummy. I am young ... uninhibited ... playing among the flowers ... sun shining brightly ... butterflies dancing around me ... exuberant joy ... a world of possibilities.

Kaleidoscope of multicoloured fractals ... soft feminine voice calling me ... enormous stone temple complex ... trees and lakes ... exquisite buildings ... heavenly nymphs carved into the walls ... "Where are we?" ... sultry sway ... 'Angkor Wat, Cambodia' ... gorgeous wink ... 'Home of the goddesses' ... walk through the five pillars ... huge door ... spacious chamber.

Gentle whisper ... 'Everything has changed' ... hands twirl sensuously ... three shimmering portals open in front of me ... 'Peek inside' ... move forward tentatively ... it's me, alone, patting a dog, on a beautiful beach, content ... next one ... blonde woman, holding hands, sharing a good life ... finally ... ravishing pink flower, long dark hair, pitter-patter of little feet, family ... 'You are ready. Your choice.'

I swallow anxiously. Walking through a graveyard. Rows upon rows of gleaming headstones. Freshly mown green grass. Bouquets and mementos. Diverse epitaphs. What makes for a good life? What will be significant in the end? How much I have achieved? How deeply I have loved? My heart stirs. I yearn for family, deep friendships and soul mates. I want to belong to a tribe.

Instantly sober. Open my eyes. Toss the mask. Swig of water. Shaman smiles, points to the door. Unsteady on my feet. Glance at the unconscious form of Bernard. Exit the house. Mother Nature embraces me, holds me, nurtures me. I love her. I love her! Hugging a tree, admiring the luminescent leaves. Tramping on fallen pine needles. What bliss! Droplets of rain drizzling over my head. Bringing sustenance to the earth. How wonderful. A Blue Mockingbird bathing in a shallow pool on a flat rock. "La - la - la - la - la!" Feel so connected. So happy!

Sitting beneath the effervescent sweet gum tree ... deluged by ecstasy ... it's all good ... drifting away.

Rough hand on my shoulder. Startled. Staring into the blurry eyes of my friend.

What's up, dude?

"Floating ..."

Yeah ...

"You done?"

Nods impassively.

How was your journey?

"Met the fear. Processed it."

Cool. What was the origin?

"My bipolar mother."

Tough childhood?

"Rough memories of my early years. Parents divorced when I was five. Father won custody of me and my sister."

Trauma requiring a psychedelic journey.

"Indeed. Optimal remedy."

The time dilation is crazy. It seems like minutes or days, yet a few hours pass.

Check my phone: 5.30pm

"Time is very different in a journey."

Wonder if Bernard wants to share.

He coughs quietly.

My trip was amazing. Golden Eagle flying through the stars. Planets whizzing past. Sense of oneness with the cosmos. Palette of brilliant colours. Profound celestial music. Spectacular.

His voice tone is mixed.

"Fantastic, bro!"

Wait a few moments.

"You seem unsatisfied."

He strokes his scalp pensively.

I feel kind of sad and lonely.

"Wounds surfacing."

Place my arm around his shoulders.

He tenses briefly, then relaxes.

"Always in your corner."

Thanks, bro.

"Shall I leave you to meditate?"

Please.

"I'll go make dinner. Call you in an hour."

Perfect.

Anyone can cook pasta. A little imagination goes a long way. Light some candles, place a few amber leaves on the table. Origami napkins. Hopefully a meal will cheer him up.

The evening is rather sedate. Bernard is probably reacquainting with a painful issue. I give him space. He trundles off to bed early. I repose on the sofa for another hour, contemplating the mysterious healing power of entheogens and the unfathomable quintessence of our shaman.

* * *

It's our day off.

Rest and recuperation.

At mid-morning there is a knock on the door.

The master surprises us with his presence.

We gather in our usual place in the warm sun.

He lays his walking stick gently on the ground.

"Focus your ears and minds. Lecture coming."

The words make me smile.

"Consider these vital components of entheogen journeys: **support** and **integration**.

"Whether you are enjoying psychedelic therapy in a psychologist's office or doing entheogen journeys with a shaman, you need to have a **support system** in place. You will be undergoing a multitude of psychological and spiritual changes. Many of your experiences will be profound, dramatic and unconventional. Part of your support system is the debrief and follow-up sessions offered by your psychologist or shaman. The other part is the sharing of your adventures with carefully selected family members, friends or fellow psychonauts.

"Integration refers to the transformation that occurs after a journey. **Internal integration** is the change of your 'inner world' (adopting new thoughts, feelings, beliefs). **External integration** is the realignment of your 'outer world' (shifting relationships, work, abode). Integration may continue for weeks or months after a journey.

"Internal integration may be accelerated or slowed depending on your attitude. It can be difficult to accept and absorb novel unconscious material and revolutionary teachings acquired during a journey. You may decide to squeeze the new information into your existing conceptual framework, to fit it into your ideological box. Ideally, of course, you should restructure your conceptual framework, remap your ideology, create a bigger box.

"External integration is the alignment of your inner and outer worlds. For some psychonauts there will be minimal changes to relationships or work. For others there will be substantive and significant changes. If your house is built on a solid foundation with structural integrity, it will remain standing after entheogen journeys. Sometimes you have to replace a wall or ceiling. Occasionally the entire house has to be rebuilt.

"Entheogen journeys generate spontaneous change. This results from the surfacing and resolution of unconscious material, the revealing and processing of perinatal and past life issues, and the experiencing of transcendent states. Although 70% of the change is natural and spontaneous, 30% is what I call 'homework'. Deep insight, catharsis and divine teachings are fabulous. However, after **awareness, acceptance** and **absorption** comes **action**! You need to implement the acquired insights and knowledge. Perhaps this means repairing or changing relationships, being kinder to yourself and others, improving your diet or treating nature with more respect. Only you know what must be done.

"As always, you have free will. You are responsible for your life. You are creating your reality."

The shaman sweeps a few leaves into his hands and throws them in the air. Varicoloured parachutes sway and dance unbelievably slowly toward the ground.

"Any questions, my protégés?"

Bernard appears rather sullen.

I want to get down to business.

"Indeed. This will be your final Ololiuqui journey. Make the most of it."

Ah. I didn't realise there was a deadline.

Ready to navigate the terrain.

He touches my shoulder.

"Alex, you stay here. This is your journey site. No eyemask. Consider your intentions. I'll be back shortly. Bernard, come with me."

They amble to the house.

Hmm … intentions … fear … claustrophobia … freedom.

Notice a shift in the atmosphere. Strange presences.

Wish I could see other-dimensional beings.

Oh yeah … clear my energy.

Seal it in Light.

Ready to rock 'n roll.

Here comes my drink.

Waiting … waiting … waiting … Feel so relaxed out here. Trees are twinkling. Birdsong caressing my ears. Warm and cosy. Huge influx of energy. Wow. Nature is conversing with me. 'Grows, blossoms, withers, dies. Rhythm of life. Aether is eternal.'

"What is aether?"

'The fifth element that underlies all creation.'

Soft mist swirling around me. A vortex is forming. 'What are you waiting for?'

Shrug insouciantly. "I am content. Why should I move?"

Dark eyes menacing. 'You are running out of time.'

Oh my God. I can't breathe. Thick pulsing walls enfolding me. Squashing me. Oh no! Not this! Please God. Where is the shaman? Being strangled by a fluid cocoon. 'You are not wanted! What are you doing here?' Another voice. 'You chose this! You agreed to this!'

Unbearable. What's going on? 'You asked to be born into this life. Clear karma.' Oh my! She is rejecting me. Smothering me. It's too hard. Clinging to the sides. 'Do you want this life or not?' Angry response. "Yes, I do!"

Squeezed through the darkness. Terrible pain. Resistance. Fighting back. Have to survive. Something wrapped around my throat. Must break free. "Aaargghh!" Bright, noisy, mind-shattering. Coddled. Recognise those eyes. You again. Play out the cosmic roles. You opted to be my mother. To repay your debt. Hope it works out.

Suddenly back in the forest. Almighty scream escapes. Gasping for air. Oh my God. I can breathe! I can breathe! Stroking my throat. Relief. Stumble to my feet. Swaying with delight. Arms embracing the scintillating sky. Nature's high-fidelity orchestra suffusing my soul.

Catapulted into an enormous chamber. Extravagant carvings decorate the stone walls. Regal obelisks stand guard in a wide circle. Purple robes flutter in an invisible breeze. Twelve illuminated beings surround a dazzling stream of Light. I feel disoriented and overwhelmed.

Do you think he remembers us?

"What am I doing here?"

Who are you?

"Who am I?"

What is your mission?

Sadness permeates me.

"I have lost everything. My tribe, my people. Washed away. By our arrogance, our foolishness. Then I lost my ocean. I miss my ocean. I long for dolphin clicks and whale songs."

What is your mission?

"To bring it back to Earth."

What do you need to do?

"Clear all karma."

Karma-free diamond strings.

I nod earnestly.

"Yes. The strings that connect all beings. Mine are tainted."

Sagacious scrutiny.

"Where is the Crystal Sceptre?"

You are not ready.

Roar of anger.

"Why not?"

Enough. You know what to do.

Hands flourish in unison.

Flung under the sweet gum tree.

What is happening to me?

Huge shriek from the house.

I rush over, open the front door.

Bernard sitting up, face contorted.

No! No, no, no, no!

Tears streaming.

Shaman halts me.

"Do not touch him."

Glare at the old man.

"Never interrupt the process."

Heave a big sigh. What kind of crazy journeys are these? How can I stand here and watch? Too much … information … emotion … energy.

Sense the light touch on my forehead. Suddenly dizzy. Laid out on the couch. Soft blanket. Serenity enfolds me.

Footsteps. Creaking floorboard. Open my eyes.

"Bernard?"

Right here, bro.

"What time is it?"

7pm

"What are you doing?"

Making dinner. Starving.

Prop myself on an elbow. Ruffle my hair.

"You ok, dude? Heard you crying."

Floodgates. Grief. Long overdue.

"How you feeling?"

Peaceful. Tender.

"Need a hug?"

Not right now.

"Cool. Where's the shaman?"

Hands me the note: 'See you in a few days. CS.'

"Wow. I have questions."

You know what he would say.

"Experience before ideology?"

Sacrosanct motto.

Scratch my cheek.

"Recuperation is welcome. I'm exhausted."

Yeah … my soul has been wrung.

"Guess we'll take it easy tonight."

Suits me, bro. Fuel up, lay down.

"Support and integration."

The evening wafts away.

Sleep embraces us.

* * *

We fill the week with short bike rides, grocery shopping, walks in the town, hiking in the woods, throwing the flying disc, under-tree meditation and long periods of contemplation.

Three Ololiuqui journeys have given much to integrate. Challenging ideas and novel concepts, revelatory unconscious material, emotional catharsis and radical spiritual experiences.

Perhaps it is the fourth day when Bernard's energy finally settles. His vigour and sparkle are returning. I notice a spring in his step.

We are seated outside eating sandwiches.

"You're looking cheerful, dude."

Definitely. Feel much better.

"Pulled out a few thorns."

He nods thoughtfully.

Hurts when extracted but worth it.

"It's weird revisiting the experiences."

Recapturing the journey events?

"Yeah. Stretches the mind."

Expands your consciousness.

"Way beyond."

You never shared your last experience.

Scratching my head tentatively.

"You were reticent about your star seed and off-world adventures. Perhaps because I have been neutral or sceptical about spiritual matters. Now it's my turn. I can barely cope with what I have seen."

Disarming smile.

Open mind. No judgement.

Scrunch my lips.

"I lived in Atlantis."

Awesome! Tell me more.

"My body was equally adept on land and in water. When the cataclysm wiped out our nation, many of us continued to live comfortably under the oceans and seas. Ego and arrogance tainted the strings of light that connect us with other beings. Sadly, I accrued karma. Subsequent incarnations also took me away from my beloved ocean."

Phew. A multitude of losses.

"I love water. Adore being immersed in it. Yet I have a fear of drowning."

How interesting.

"Met supremely powerful beings during the journey. Advised me to clear my karma."

Uh oh.

"I need to attain crystal clear strings of light. They call these 'diamond strings'."

Cool epithet.

"Also processed a traumatic birth experience. Entry into my current life."

Your mother again?

"Yeah. We seem energetically entwined."

Have you forgiven her?

"Uh … no."

The long way of expunging karma is through multiple incarnations with varied roles and scripts. The short way is through forgiveness.

"Equally difficult strategies."

Diminishing ego and increasing love.

"Challenging for anyone."

Bernard shrugs casually.

Remember the words of our shaman.

"You are creating your reality."

Another sacrosanct motto.

"Dude, you are annoyingly wise."

A broad smile creases his face.

Integration consolidates knowledge.

"Anything you wish to share?"

A cascade of grief and tears.

"Your entire journey?"

Yeah. Much needed.

"Good for you."

I place my hands behind my head and flop backwards onto the soft leaves. Blue sky shimmers through the psychedelic treetops. Warm sun nuzzles my neck. I laugh freely. A few more days of rest and we'll be ready for the next journey.

* * *

It is pouring with rain outside. Nowhere to go, nothing to do.

When the front door opens, revealing our bedraggled shaman, it is a welcome relief.

I peruse him suspiciously. There is not a drop of water on his clothes. Even his boots are dry.

He raises his hands amiably.

"How are my protégés?"

All good this morning.

I nod cordially.

"Ready for the next level?"

Oh yeah. Bring it on.

The shaman reaches into his bag, unfolds his palm and reveals a troop of mushrooms.

"The Mazatec use the Nahuatl word **Teonanacatl** (*pronounced Teao-nahnah-cut*) for this entheogen. Teo means 'God, divine, sacred'; nacatl means 'body, flesh'; nanacatl means 'fungus, mushroom'. Hence, the colloquial term is 'sacred mushroom' or 'God's flesh'.

"**Psilocybin mushrooms** (aka psychedelic mushrooms, magic mushrooms or shrooms) are mushrooms that contain the psychedelic compounds **psilocybin** and **psilocin**. There are over 200 species of psilocybin mushrooms distributed across the continents of this planet. More than 50 species are found in Mexico. Psilocybin mushroom identification, gathering and preparation for consumption should only be done by a shaman, botanist or mushroom expert as many species of mushrooms are poisonous.

"Teonanacatl has been used for thousands of years in Mesoamerica and across the planet. In prehistoric Europe they consumed *Psilocybe semilanceata* (aka liberty cap), one of the world's most prolific and potent magic mushrooms. In North America, Asia and Europe they consumed *Amanita muscaria* (aka fly agaric or fly amanita), a distinctly recognisable red mushroom with white spots. In Mesoamerica the Mexica (Aztec), the Maya and their predecessors used *Psilocybe mexicana* and *Psilocybe semperviva*.

"My preferred Teonanacatl is *Psilocybe semperviva* (aka *Psilocybe hoogshagenii*). This mushroom is found in the states of Puebla, Oaxaca and Chiapas, where it grows at elevations of 1,000-1,800 metres. The name derives from Latin, semper meaning 'always, forever, eternally' and viva meaning 'living'. This sacred mushroom is living eternally. Colloquial names for this mushroom include 'little birds of the woods' and 'the children'.

"When used as an entheogen Teonanacatl can be ingested whole or finely ground and enjoyed as a tea. Ideally mushrooms are consumed on an empty stomach. Mushroom tea, especially with a squeeze of citrus juice, results in quicker onset (within 15 minutes). Journeys take place in quiet darkness and last 4-6 hours depending on dosage. Effects include close- and open-eye visuals, synaesthesia, altered sense of time, novel thought processes, profound insights, euphoria, dying of self, meeting with higher beings, immersion in the Light."

The Crystal Shaman engages his penetrating stare.

"What more do you need to know?"

I shrug genially.

Bernard strokes his chin.

Any journey advice?

He smiles enigmatically.

"Psilocybin mushrooms often give rise to intense mystical and transcendent events. These can be the most profound spiritual and psychological experiences of your life. Your perception, and therefore your reality, may shift dramatically. Depression, trauma, anxiety and existential loneliness often dissipate. Your consciousness may connect to All That Is. You may finally understand the eternal Now. You may revel in ecstasy; however, you may also have moments of feeling you are too weak for the ordeal, you are going crazy, or you are dying."

Wow. New terrain to navigate.

"Remember your tools: witness, breathe, surrender. Try to accept whatever transpires. Resistance only makes the journey harder. Replace fear with avid curiosity. Embrace the visions and revelations no matter how profound or painful."

Darn it. Here come those butterflies again.

"Tell me about your breakfast."

Just granola, two hours ago.

"No protein, pure carbs?"

I nod in agreement.

"Perfect."

He goes to the kitchen and brews two mushroom teas. Adds a squeeze of lime. Then points to the sofas.

"Set your intentions now."

Try to calm my nerves. Let me think ... clear karma ... diamond strings.

Glance across at Bernard's composed face.

Shaman hands us our drinks.

"Travel well, brother."

And you, bro.

Water bottle nearby. Eyemask on. Here we go.

Few minutes pass. Strange sensation. Immersed in a golden-white fractal. Disorientating. Morphs into a brightly coloured vortex. Huge neon pink-and-green snake slithering past. Invites me to follow. I am scared. What's waiting for me? Breathe ... breathe ... uh ... what was the advice ... avid curiosity ... let go ... surrender ...

Dressed in a long robe. Bare feet. Pale skin, black hair. My name is Mark Dumont. Catholic priest in Paris, France. Standing on the edge of a lake or river. Cannot see behind me. Arms bound to a heavy block. Why am I so different to my brothers? Why do I know things that people conceal? Why do other-dimensional beings converse with me? Ritual and incantation. My brothers push me backward. Not fearful. *Splash!* I love water. The beings will intervene. Can't breathe. No air. Struggling. Help me! Help me! Shaking. No, no, no! Dim light receding above me.

Eyes open. Gasping for air. Massive influx of energy. Laughter grips me. Tears of relief. It's gone! My fear of drowning is gone. I blink slowly. Engulfed by radiant light. A woman stands before me. 'What did you learn? What will you do now?' Survey the glistening white mist lapping my ankles. "Ignorance and spirituality lead to harm. Keep myself safe. Be alone." She gently pats me on the head. 'Are you sure?' Golden Eagle swooping … strong wings beating the air … *Be real. Be free. Forgive.* Oh yeah. Turn back to the woman. "Uh … I need to be me … who I truly am … no matter what is happening … uh … I forgive my brothers … clear the strings … no more reincarnation and roles … only love flows toward them …"

In the forest. Meet the alpha wolf. 'Well done, El lobo.' Running through the trees. Full moon riding high. Pack howling vociferously. Smiling. I belong. I belong. Sense the creaking of a branch. Notice the huge psychedelic snake coiled in a tree. 'Waiting for you … work to do.'

Nature swirling … snow on the ground … in the distance a monastery … such peace … meditating by a waterfall … in Tibet … my name is Alim Raheb … the teacher is levitating above me … shares pure truth … different to the doctrine and laws of the monks … 'Fasting is a waste of time; feed your brain with knowledge and food' … the imperativeness of love … 'It is one of the purest and most beautiful energies' … he disappears and reappears at will … teaches no one but me … I am unpopular with the monks … they often startle me when I am meditating.

In deep contemplation … mind flowing in hallowed dimensions … unaware of my body … rope slipped around my neck … hanged from a tree … wake … struggle … can't breathe! … no, no, no, no! … such a beautiful life … sad to depart … three monks below … recognise their essences … mother … friend … compatriot.

Luminescent glow suffusing the sacred scenery. Soft mist curling around my legs. The woman stands before me again. 'Thoughts?

Conclusions?' Hmm ... "Break the pattern ... no longer hide ... accept my uniqueness ... shine my light ... seek advanced spiritual beings ... find my tribe ... um ... I forgive my mother ... forgive all the monks ... clear the strings ... no more anger, sadness, holding on ... it's their karma ... I am done."

I am at a party ... rainbow balloons ... jubilance ... many beings applauding ... 'Welcome home, Alex!' ... 'Congratulations!' ... 'Good to see you!' ... 'Whoo hoo!' ... enormous vortex opening ... 'Go play ... enjoy yourself!' ... leap into pulsating waves ... colossal water slide ... sun is shining ... air is fresh and invigorating ... I am me! ... I am free! ... I can breathe! ... *Splash!* ... into the cool sea ... tears of joy ... sweet memories cascading ... dolphins cavorting and clicking ... ah ... my birthplace ... my origin ... my home.

Eyes flutter open ... candles flickering ... crane my neck ... my friend is unmoving ... shaman quietly clapping ... surreal ... stretch my arms ... yawn ... lurch to my feet ... head to the door. Oh ... Wow! ... Mother Nature is ravishing ... elegant ... loving ... nurturing ... meandering through the tranquil trees ... tossing leaves high ... crackling pine needles underfoot ... singing to the delightful birds ... filled with rapturous joy.

An hour later Bernard stumbles outside.

Sheesh! That was wild.

"Past lives?"

How'd you know?

"Happened to me."

May I share?

"Sure."

I was a Roman soldier … military service was compulsory … enjoyed the training and camaraderie … but conflicted with my essence … ordered to execute people in a cave … saw a hovering basketball-shaped light … reminded me of my true nature … absconded … became a hermit … spent rest of life in meditation, reflection and solitude … deep tranquillity.

"What was the learning?"

Spirituality is paramount. Stay true to myself.

I nod affably.

Another life … in England … inheritance … library in my house … lent out books for money … long walks in nearby woods … met extra-terrestrial beings … small, grey, big eyes … missing time … confused … can't discuss with anyone … became isolated … died alone.

"Sad story."

The debrief showed me the importance of spiritual discernment. Connecting only with beings of love and light. Seeking advanced altruistic souls. Locating my tribe.

"Did you say 'tribe'?"

Yeah, dude. For too long the children of the stars have walked alone on this Earth. As have the Atlanteans and neo-Egyptians. The cosmic races, crystal people and stone people need to come out of the shadows. Celestial energy is arriving. Change is coming. We need to unite and rise up against the darkness.

"Where did that come from?"

The words tumbled out my mouth.

Crystal Shaman is striding toward us.

Raises a firm hand.

"It is dangerous to speak of such things. First finish your healing and consolidate your power. Then you can quietly join the movement."

Bernard stares in astonishment.

"You both have a mission. That is why you are my protégés. You carry the mark. Focus on clearing your energy and karma. Enter the portals. Master the higher dimensions."

We are stupefied and silent.

The shaman is glimmering. Hazy. Indistinct. Form changing. Alpha wolf. Sudden growl and snarl. Circles us once. Runs into the forest.

No way, man.

"Whoa. It's all true."

Alex! Alex!

"What is it?"

Your hair is standing up.

Teeth feel weird. Body tremoring.

"It's ok, dude. Everything is alright."

Are we still journeying?

"Nope. This is real."

Radical. Shape-shifter.

"Preternatural."

Mind blown.

Is it the stress? The shock? We both fall to the ground, rolling with laughter. Maybe it's the only natural response. Maybe it's a complete system reset.

We spend the evening and next day pondering and assimilating. Interspersed with rest, recuperation and tasty meals. I am grateful to be away from regular life. These are optimal conditions for uninterrupted metamorphosis.

* * *

We are sitting in the lounge anxiously awaiting the arrival of the shaman. There are many questions. It's time to unravel the enigma and reveal the truth.

He appears at midday. Places his bag on the table. Nods amicably.

I launch into it straight away.

"You became a wolf. How?"

Shrugs insouciantly.

"The Sun is shining infinite rays of light. You are a point of consciousness on one of those rays of light. **Your position dictates your perception which dictates your reality**. If you shift your awareness, in other words move along your particular ray, you will discover things currently hidden from you. In more advanced work, you can jump onto other rays."

Hmm. I've heard that before.

"You have already experienced shifts in awareness. When you met in the forest as a wolf and an eagle. That occurred as you jumped onto other rays."

Bernard blurts an interjection.

Was that a shared hallucination?

"Hallucination is a shift in perception. Perception dictates reality."

I don't understand. What is real?

The shaman laughs softly.

"Everything is Consciousness. From one perspective, the universe is an interconnected network of consciousness, every being linked to every other being. From another perspective, the universe consists of layers of consciousness or multi-dimensions. From a higher vantage point, you understand the universe as rays of the Sun or emanations of God or radiances of the Source. Ultimately, however, you will discover there is only one Consciousness."

My friend thoughtfully strokes his chin.

Perhaps we need another line of inquiry.

"You mentioned that sacred mushrooms have been used for thousands of years in Mesoamerica and across the planet."

His inscrutable gaze is mesmerising.

"When the gods left the Earth, teacher plants remained as gateways and portals to higher dimensions. From the psychoactive blue lotus (*Nymphaea caerulea*) and mandrake herb

(*Mandragora officinarum*) used by the Egyptians, to the white water lily (*Nymphaea ampla*), sacred mushrooms and extensive psychedelic pharmacopoeia used by the Maya and their predecessors, to the ergot-based LSD-like potion called the kykeon that was consumed at the Eleusinian Mysteries in Greece, to the secretive soma in India, to the psychoactive brew ayahuasca of the Amazonian Indians. There are numerous and diverse entheogens spread across this world."

What do you mean by 'gods'?

The shaman gives an esoteric wink.

"That is a whole other story. Truth is, beings manifest in a multitude of ways. Some physical and highly advanced compared to humans. Some ethereal and invisible to the human eye. Many are located on faraway planets. Most are able to travel in the multi-dimensions.

"As my old friend Śakra taught, 'These dimensions are not layers but expressions of Life. Hence they manifest in countless ways. Your perception limits you to the terms 'physical' and 'spiritual'. Life, however, expresses itself in unlimited configurations and forms.'

"Secrets have been hidden for thousands of years within abstruse texts, cryptic rituals, and the inner sanctum of mysterious orders. Gateways to higher consciousness and transcendence have been closely guarded. Portals to the multi-dimensions and beings of light have been astutely concealed. Now the resonance is shifting. Shamans, spiritual teachers, enlightened guides, extraterrestrial entities and other-dimensional beings are revealing the truth.

"Cosmic forces are aligning with Earthly forces. The dark lattice is going to be destroyed. The human race is approaching an evolutionary jump. Finally, it is time for the shift."

Can you explain more about shamanism?

"A psychonaut journeys to acquire healing and knowledge for himself. A shaman journeys to acquire healing and knowledge for other people. Shamans enter the cosmic portals, navigate the multi-dimensions, interact with higher beings and return with gifts for their tribe.

"Shamanism cannot be learned by studying a book or doing a series of seminars. You cannot enrol in a university or college. It is not a system of rituals and incantations that you need to master. It does not require special devices or tools.

"You become a shaman only by travelling the multi-dimensions, building your navigation skills and having the courage to penetrate deeper and deeper into the Unknown. Over time awareness shifts along and across the rays of light.

"Shamans usually have a 'calling', a strong drawing to the arcane and mysterious. In truth, they carry the 'mark', a distinctive energy resonance entwined in their soul. If you have the mark, you usually experience the deepest fulfilment when you work as a shaman. You may, of course, choose to ignore the mark and live an ordinary life.

"It is not easy becoming a shaman. All your learning takes place through entheogen journeys. The other-dimensional beings expect the forfeiture of lower-order energy and consciousness in exchange for higher-order energy and consciousness. This can be painful and uncomfortable. Often it means the loss of all you cherish and possess in order to receive knowledge and power. Ascending the Sacred Ladder requires commitment, courage, humility, surrender and trust. The Sacred Ladder cannot hold the weight of human ego and limited ideology. You need to gradually accept and embrace all the beings and concepts you encounter. Sacred journeys may be gentle, ecstatic, profound, challenging or overwhelming.

"Not all higher-dimensional beings are welcoming or interested in visitors. Some blatantly ignore you or merely tolerate your presence. Others assist with loving-kindness and teachings. A few may mentor you. You learn to navigate to the optimal realms."

I sigh pensively.

Bernard glances at me.

Shall we get on with it?

"Yeah. I'm ready."

We clear and seal the energy fields. Check eyemasks. Water nearby.

The shaman brews our mushroom teas and adds a squeeze of lime.

Quick quaff, get comfortable, settle the mind, focus on intentions.

These journeys require steely courage. Whatever is buried or partially hidden becomes dramatically exposed. You have no choice but to confront your quirks, issues, traumas and shadows. It is wonderful having thorns removed but it can leave you disoriented. Who are you when your issues dissolve? When your cherished beliefs and self-concepts disappear?

Head is woozy. Feeling of uneasiness.

Onslaught of brilliant yellow fractals.

Stay calm … breathe … breathe …

Enormous brightly coloured vortex … huge ruby-emerald snake … 'Remember me?' Moment of anxiety. Why is this so scary? Witness … aha … snake with feathers … never noticed before …

'Come' … I hesitate … oh my … witness … breathe … surrender … enter the vortex …

Egyptian hieroglyphs cover the walls … fabulous stone work … cryptic markers … they have a secret … must find it … determined … want to be powerful again … into the pyramid … many tunnels … decisions … know it's here somewhere … move quickly … access another tunnel … door rushes down behind me … sand spurting from the walls … not enough fresh air … moving forward … tunnel getting narrow … no way back … slipping down … wedged into stone … arms trapped … unable to move … oh no … no, no, no! … mouth parched … hours pass … panic … struggle … no fight left … unconscious.

Woman with long dark hair … radiant mist ebbing and flowing … she touches my chest gently … 'Let it go, let it go' … screaming … weight lifting from me … tears falling … relief … I can breathe … freedom suffusing my body … oh … my claustrophobia is gone … gone! … I am free … I am free!

Hissing and flapping. Sense of urgency. 'Go now.' Luminescent portal shimmering before me … friendly shove … propelled through black starry heavens … land on the summit of a pyramid-temple … the Maya … sacrificial blade in my hand … prisoner is naked and painted blue … enemy priest … stretched over the convex stone … time to take his power … stare into his eyes … hear the curse *Your throat will close. You will not breathe.* Ignore it … blade descends … decapitated … head rolls down the temple steps … roar from crowd below … suddenly gripped by his eyes … pools reflecting back at me … oh my … it's Bernard … no … my heart is crushed … no! … press my palms to my face … What have I done? … entwining thread of light … bonded by a curse … souls of similar resonance … on my knees … "Please forgive me. Please forgive me."

Star seed ascending the stone steps … slowly approaching … grips my forearm … *It's enough, brother. Karma must end.* Eyes locking onto mine. *We are spiritual warriors. Lessons are learned. Let's fulfil our mission.* I nod earnestly. "Will you forgive me?" Poignant pause. *Done.* Pull him into a hug. Patting his back. "I forgive you too."

Quietude settles. Overwhelmed by flashing images. Arrogance and egotism in Atlantis. Crystal sceptre. Losing my power. Expelled from the ocean. Trying to regain power in Mesoamerica and Egypt. Trapped and suffocating in a pyramid. Hanged from a tree. Drowned. Struggling in a birth canal. Claustrophobia. Breathing issues. Fear. Carrying the mark. Spiritually advanced. Dissimilar to priests and monks. Alone. Mistrustful. Isolated. Lost.

Soothing feminine energy ... 'What's the lesson?' Hmm ... diamond strings ... impeccability ... respect ... love ... kindness ... altruism ... "It must be love." Caressing my crown chakra. 'Are you ready to forgive yourself?' I am crying. I don't know how. It's harder to forgive myself than forgive others.

Standing on the apex of a pyramid ... all my lifetimes swirling around me ... sensing this crucial moment ... shaking with apprehension ... darkness above ... raising my hands ... "I forgive myself ... I forgive myself ... I forgive myself for every lifetime ... I forgive myself for everything!" An enormous bolt of lightning cascades through my existence ... igniting my consciousness ... the heavens vibrate ... psychedelic rainbows dance in the skies ... celestial exultations ... The scintillating woman peruses me proudly. 'Karma is expunged. Finish your last lesson.'

I am sitting on the sofa. Head in hands. Eyemask tossed to one side. Feelings of relief and joy flooding through me. My old life has been erased. I know who I am. Understand my essence. Forgiveness and freedom. Able to create my life as I choose.

Bernard stirs. Opens his eyes. Looks directly at me.

That was real, brother. I understand now.

He places his fist on his heart.

Love you, man.

Tears burn my cheeks.

"Love you too, bro."

We have a great life ahead of us.

Tipping point. Sobbing. Everything is changing.

Blow my nose. Scrutinise the empty chair.

Where in the world is our shaman?

Lively conversation late into the evening.

At midnight we finally lay heads on pillows.

The last thing I do is smile and surrender.

What dreams may come.

* * *

The Crystal Shaman arrives two days later. We probably needed the extra time to integrate our powerful journeys. Our minds have been stretched and ideologies shattered. Past the point of no return. All we can do is accept and embrace the new concepts and teachings.

I notice the solemn countenance.

"This will be your final mushroom journey. Breakthroughs beckon."

Here come the butterflies again.

Bernard raises his hand uncertainly.

We have dealt with past lives and karma. What's left?

The shaman bursts into jovial laughter.

"How you vibrate the connecting strings effects all other beings. Hence, the value of impeccability, altruism and radical respect. Diamond strings are a vital step. Now it's time to raise your resonance.

"Consciousness is a resonance. You cannot give it a name and identity. If you do, you limit it immediately and it stagnates. You are a fleeting thought of God. A thought of God that becomes self-aware then desperately tries to preserve its 'aliveness'.

"How much are you willing to let go? What will be asked of you during your journey? To say goodbye to your beliefs, stories, ideologies, achievements, connections, ego, identity, entire life? Are you ready to die to self and be born again as Self? How terrifying would that be? How glorious? How ecstatic?"

Large butterflies dancing in my tummy.

The mushroom teas are brewing.

Clear the energy. Seal in Light.

My intention is: surrender.

Spiritual warriors, dude!

"Yeah. Let's do it."

Trepidation subsides.

Drink the tea. Deep breaths. Try to relax.

Waiting. Waiting. Shivering. Body cold. Extra blanket.

Rush of wings. Voices talking. 'Is he ready?' 'Survivor. Fighter.' 'Will he let go?' Massive influx of energy. Catapulted into the stratosphere. Zero support. Out of control. Falling. Falling. No! Must protect myself. Ground rapidly approaching. Impact imminent. Black hole. Descending. Crash onto eerie landscape. Smokey. Bare trees burned by fire. Scorched earth. Desolation.

Walking through blackened shrubs. Glance at my legs. Flesh peeling, bones protruding. What is happening? Further on, lying on its side, my crushed motorbike. Hours pass slowly. Crackling voice. 'Why do you think you are special? What is your life worth?' All the books I have read, burning in a pile. Photographs of relationships crisping and curling. Hands are ugly. Body is skeletal. It's the end of me. Weeping. Can't do this anymore. No strength. "I don't want to die."

Gleaming light in the distance. Crawling on elbows and knees. In a clearing, a colossal multicoloured tree. Dozens of strings hanging from every branch. Each string suspending a black or white crescent-shaped face. Tree of Life. The faces are diametric opposites, diverse perceptual positions, varying roles. Stern voice. 'Anything you exclude disconnects you from the totality of Consciousness.'

Swept up by a monstrous wave. Exhausted. Beings floating above me. 'Lower consciousness yearns to be absorbed by higher consciousness. Higher consciousness intends to subsume lower consciousness.' Sinking to the ocean floor. My bedroom in Oregon. I open the chest of drawers. Extract an ethereal box. Here is my brief marriage. The beings snub me. Open the second drawer. Here is a passionate past-life relationship. 'Give that to us.' I recoil slightly. "That is precious to me."

Assessing. Calibrating. Holding tightly onto my beliefs. Trying to keep my stories intact. My memories define who I am. Or do they? Grasping for the navigation tools. Witness … breathe … uh …

I am a tiny drop immersed in an enormous ocean. Why am I alone? Why am I separate? Soft feminine presence. 'Surrender to us. Be with us.' Trickle of fear. Scared of dying. What lies beyond this life? Laughter ripples through the water. 'You keep yourself separate from us. Asserting your rigid boundaries. Desperately holding onto your identity.'

"I don't want to die!"

The veneer of self isolates me from All That Is.

A drop of consciousness resisting an ocean of Consciousness.

Every journey pushing the boundaries between life and Life, between illusory me and real Me, between this separate speck of consciousness and One Consciousness.

How do I know all that?

Oh yes … many tribes, One Tribe … many beings, One Being … networks of Light … layers of Consciousness … moving along the rays to the Sun … underlying Is-ness … the Source.

Why am I fighting? Why am I resisting?

I am One Consciousness. I was asleep.

I am the Creator. I am the Source.

Ecstatic. Blissful. Pulse of Life.

Eternal Here Now.

I Am.

I Am.

Eyes flitter open. Sofa, chairs, table, walls, house, shaman, friend. All One. All Me. I Am. I Am. I Am. Burst into laughter. Ah, the glorious illusion of it all. Never alone. Creator and creation. The flow of Consciousness. The breath of Life.

Eventually it all settles. Ubiquitous tranquillity remains.

Bernard has the giggles. I hear him conversing with beings of light. An hour later he emerges from his shroom cocoon. Stretches his wings. Smiles broadly.

Hey brother.

"What's good?"

Everything.

"All of Life?"

Every drop.

"You awake?"

Ha-ha-ha! Totally.

"Yeah. And me."

What do we do now?

"Whatever we like."

New adventures.

"Flow of Life."

Playtime.

The evening is peaceful and sedate. Neither of us have a care in the world. We have shed our issues, traumas and fears. Delved into and resolved past lives. Discovered hidden aspects and shadows. Absorbed higher teachings. Embraced the Light. Immersed in One Consciousness.

* * *

After our customary integration day we wake enthused and energised. Early breakfast then watch a gorgeous sun rising and twinkling through the trees. Ardent birdsong echoes through the forest. A gentle breeze is ruffling amber leaves.

The hairs on my arms are bristling.

Deep howl reverberates in the distance.

What is it, dude?

"The shaman is calling us."

How do you know?

"Trust me."

I find the backpack, grab a few snacks.

"You ready for a hike?"

Definitely.

We descend the slopes and move into a different microclimate. Lush and tropical. Reminiscent of our search for the Brown-backed Solitaire. After ninety minutes we locate our shaman.

Bernard bows respectfully.

"Good morning, my protégés. Ready for your lesson?"

He crouches and points to a leafy plant.

Is that an entheogen?

"Indeed."

What is it?

"Salvia."

Aha.

"**Salvia** (aka the Shepherdess or Diviner's Sage) is a sprawling perennial herb (*Salvia divinorum*) endemic to the humid forests of the Sierra Mazateca in the state of Oaxaca. It grows to over a metre in height, flaunting large green leaves and white flowers with purple calyces. The origin of *Salvia divinorum* is a botanical mystery. The Mazatec believe it was sent to Earth on a comet.

"*Salvia divinorum* is one of the most potent entheogenic plants. The active ingredient **Salvinorin A** is a unique dissociative psychedelic. Mazatec shamans use Salvia to induce profound visionary states of consciousness. The leaves are either chewed or made into a tea or processed then vaporised and inhaled. Smoking results in quickest onset (within 45 seconds) and the journey lasts 15-60 minutes depending on the method of ingestion. Journeys are usually done in quiet darkness.

"As with Mystic Toad DMT, you will ingest Salvia by smoking. I will apply a flame to the green powder in this glass pipe. You need to fully exhale then put your lips to the pipe and fully inhale. Hold the smoke in your lungs as long as possible. Then you will enter Salvia world."

Are we doing it right here?

The shaman shrugs.

"Why not? The sacred plant enjoys company."

I volunteer to go first. The butterflies are absent.

Familiar routine. Clear the energy. Seal in Light.

Place my jacket on the moist ground. Sit comfortably.

Here we go. Exhale. Deep inhale. Hold it. Hold it.

Something has shifted. Where am I? Who am I? Memories are gone. Pushing through a viscous membrane. Unusual landscape. Presences. Awaiting my arrival. Greeting. Not language but a thought-force permeating my being. Orientating myself. Everything seems familiar. Been here before. Numerous times.

The space between lifetimes. Souls ponder their experiences. Mentored by higher beings. Prepare for reincarnation.

No thoughts, concepts or memories. Immediacy of consciousness. Pure awareness.

Question emanates as an energetic ripple.

"Why am I here?"

You have a living physical body on Earth. You breached the boundary of the worlds. Only advanced monks, shamans and sorcerers visit under such conditions.

"What do you mean?"

Physical body normally has to die before you enter this realm.

Flux of disruptive waves. Distorting my vision.

"What's happening?"

Commence singing.

Hear my voice uttering a rhythmic melody.

Verdant greenery. Shaman gazing proudly. Friend furrowing brow.

"Singing will weave you back into this reality."

My body is seated against a tree.

Slowly reconnect to Earth.

Grey-haired whisper.

"There is no physical tolerance to Salvia. You can engage in immediate consecutive sessions."

Ah, thinking. Slow compared to a thought-force.

Enthusiastic gesticulation.

"Need to return. Barely past an introduction."

Glass pipe approaches my mouth. Exhale. Inhale. Pause.

Welcome back.

Beckoning me to follow.

Transition of scenery. Intricate, complex topography.

Regal entity on throne. Golden crown. White undulating hair. Long golden sceptre with large translucent crystal on top. Water ebbing and flowing around his feet.

You are not ready, my child.

Tilt my head, blinking uncertainly.

One final lesson. And your power shall return.

I nod in agreement.

"Love."

Indeed.

"Altruism."

Conquer Love. Then you will lead again.

Protracted silence.

"How can I return to this place?"

Tapped firmly on the head with the crystal.

You incarnated on Earth for a reason. You have a mission. Your life is not about surfing the multi-dimensions. It is about leading your people. It is about the rise of Atlantis.

Waves crashing against my body. Wonderful exhilarating feelings. Dolphins clicking and whales singing. Suffusing my consciousness. Overwhelming joy.

Plant leaves hanging in my face. Standing. Arms outstretched. Dizzy. Is that my voice? What's happening?

Shaman grabs me as I start to fall.

Slow return to physical world.

Rest for a long while.

Bernard's smiling face.

Hey dude. Wha-a-a-t?

Mumble. Clear my throat.

"Surreal, far out, radical."

Any suggestions?

"It's the land of the dead. No precedents. Just flow."

Notice the eyes widening.

Place my hand on his shoulder.

"It's amazing, dude. You'll be alright."

He sits on my jacket. Closes his eyes.

Deep breath. Exhale. Inhale. Unmoving.

Head lolls. Smoke escapes his mouth.

Weird being the outside observer. Is anything occurring?

Twenty minutes later Bernard is slurring anxiously.

Send me back. Send me back!

Another big draw on the pipe.

He completes five journeys in two hours.

After a leisurely recovery he is ready to share.

Tears are welling in his eyes.

Met my parents and sister. And higher beings. Reunited. A family once more!

Crying. Hand him a tissue.

So good to see them. Proud of my accomplishments. Pleased with my journeys and healing. Admonished me to stop running and start living. Reminded me of the profundity of love. Said I had one final lesson then I should return to San Francisco and live my life. I need to integrate all the teachings into my current existence. It's time to live and love!

A smile dashes across my face.

There is a grand plan operating behind the scenes. Who is orchestrating all this? Perhaps that zany waitress near Area 51 was right. 'When you have a clear destination, the universe will conspire to support you.' Maybe it relates to the teaching of our shaman. 'Cosmic forces are aligning with Earthly forces. The dark lattice is going to be destroyed. The human race is approaching an evolutionary jump. Finally, it is time for the shift.' Is there a divine itinerary?

Bernard gets to his feet. Grabs the shaman into an impassioned hug.

Thank you so much. Beyond gratitude.

Then he bows deferentially.

Notice the shifting energy.

We walk back to the house.

Feel sadness in my heart.

"It's goodbye, isn't it?"

The gnarled walking stick slaps my leg.

"Our souls are strongly entwined."

I scrutinise the old man curiously.

"Some things are hidden in plain sight."

Shrug indifferently. I have no idea.

"Tomorrow is our last meeting. Prepare your questions."

He turns away, meanders through the trees.

I watch him suspiciously.

Wonder if he really needs that walking stick.

We spend the afternoon relaxing and contemplating our profound journeys. Astounding transformation has occurred under the guidance of the Crystal Shaman. Deep appreciation cascades through my soul.

Long discussions over a scrumptious dinner. An early night. My head is restless on the pillow. Tomorrow is our final chance to unravel the enigma and reveal the truth.

* * *

He arrives early the next morning.

Invites us to sit under the resplendent sweet gum tree.

"My protégés, your journeys with me are finished. The teachings are complete. How you proceed is up to you. Remember, you are creating your reality by your perceptions, choices and beliefs."

Position dictates perception which dictates reality.

"Indeed. Your position on the rays of light."

Is that the assemblage point?

"Yes. When you shift your assemblage point, or your position on the rays of light, you assemble another reality. This is not an illusion or hallucination; you are assembling another world."

What is the best way to shift the assemblage point?

"The two greatest movers of the assemblage point are entheogens and intent."

What was the rule? Faith guides intention. Intention guides energy.

Does that mean we depend on entheogens?

The Crystal Shaman throws his head back and laughs. Rises to his feet. Discards the walking stick. He is glimmering. Hazy. Indistinct. Form changing. A youthful vigorous man stands before us. Long dark hair. Eyes the colour of the sky. I am neither shocked nor surprised. His robe transforms into pure white with a blue mantle. Appears very familiar. Ache in my heart. I peruse the gnarled walking stick laying near me. It has a solid knob at the top with peculiar engravings.

Bernard is staring with astonishment.

Uh … this is really happening.

"Entheogens and intent are utilised to shift the assemblage point. This is a gradual process requiring dedication, time and patience. Once the assemblage point is stabilised in a new position, you operate in a different reality. You no longer need entheogens."

My friend is pensively rubbing his chin.

How will you shift back to an old man?

"Intent is the prime mover."

Understood.

The shaman reverts his form.

How does intent work?

"It begins with a simple repeated command. As you become adept, a single thought or key word suffices."

Is your reality very different to ours?

"My vantage point is higher."

I am beginning to understand the secrets of the shaman. It has taken a long time. His teachings are finally making sense to me. A strange sensation stirs within my soul.

He raises open palms.

"Last question."

My brow furrows.

Final pointers?

"You both carry the mark of a shaman. Avoid alcohol, nicotine, caffeine and recreational drugs. Walk with impeccability, altruism and radical respect. Never react with fear or anger. Keep the diamond strings. Establish healthy habits. Practice will and intent. Fall deeply into Love."

Bernard and I stand and bow respectfully.

The Crystal Shaman bows in return.

"Well done, my protégés. Spend the rest of the day integrating. Leave tomorrow morning. Safe travels."

He turns and ambles into the forest.

We hear the deep reverberating howls.

A friendly voice echoes in my mind.

'Until we meet again.'

* * *

We know our journey is not finished. A divine plan is surely unfolding. In the meantime, Bernard convinces me to take a trip to Palenque and Chichen Itza to see the sacred ruins.

The GPS indicates an 8-hour ride to Palenque so we set off early and arrive in the evening. We easily locate a decent hotel. The following day we revel in the spectacular sights. Palenque's architecturally sophisticated stone temples are immersed in a jungle of cedar, mahogany and sapodilla trees. We amble through the lush vegetation, admiring the beautiful Temple of the

Inscriptions, Temple of the Sun, Temple of the Count, Temple of the Cross and Temple of the Foliated Cross.

My friend is elated and enrapt.

Another 8-hour ride takes us to Chichen Itza in Yucatan State. There are plenty of hotels. We savour a tasty dinner and rest our weary bodies. The next day we tour the ruins at Chichen Itza, the large Pre-Contact Maya city that is now a UNESCO World Heritage Site. We visit the intriguing Temple of Warriors and the Great Ball Court. Then climb the steps of El Castillo (aka Temple of Kukulcan, which roughly translates as 'feathered serpent') and enjoy the breathtaking views. After half an hour Bernard requests additional time to meander among the ruins. I opt to stay at the summit and wait for his return.

Sipping the cool water from my backpack. Basking in the warm sun. Gentle breeze ruffling my shirt. Glance down the stone steps. A woman is ascending. I notice the gorgeous pink flower in her long dark hair. It is *Dahlia pinnata,* the national flower of Mexico. My mind flashes back to the daydream. Heart jumps. Could it be?

I extend my hand and help her up. Her brown eyes lock onto mine. "In Lak'ech Ala K'in." Oh my. That's not Spanish. She giggles coyly. "It's a Mayan greeting meaning 'I am another yourself' or 'I am you and you are me'."

"A beautiful salutation."

"May I sit with you?"

"Of course."

"I am Rosario Flores. Call me Rosa."

"Alexander Huxley."

She shakes her head.

"Your energy has recently shifted. You are Sasha."

Strangely, that feels right. Wait a minute. What did that zany waitress near Area 51 predict?

Serene ambience. Our resonances are conversing.

Her hand softly touches mine.

"You do know we are kindred spirits?"

Powerful feelings coursing through me.

"My soul knows. My mind is saying *Wha-a-a-t?*"

Euphoria illuminates her face.

"I want my life to be a heaven, sing to the flowers, sculpt a chakra garden, make love on a tree top, do yoga under water, make music with crystals, paint the cosmos on my naked body, shape a home with such high frequency that only pure hearts can listen."

"Wow. I would like to build that dream with you."

"Do you want a family?"

"Absolutely."

Uh oh. Here comes Bernard. This is going to be interesting.

Hey bro. Leave you alone … What happened?

Raise my hands and shrug.

"I think I got married."

Seriously?

Laughter grips me.

Rosa introduces herself.

"Lovely to meet you, Bernard."

My brow furrows. I didn't mention his name.

"I am the Crystal Shaman's daughter."

Whoa. I did not see that one coming.

We are both staring at her.

Eventually Bernard speaks.

Why are you here?

She smiles sweetly.

"Final lesson in the itinerary."

You will teach us about love?

"In a sense."

At this temple?

"Are you aware of the date?"

Mmm. Must be late December.

"Three days until Christmas."

Oh yeah. Lost track of time.

She places her hand gently on Bernard's shoulder.

"You're going to love Tulum. It's a resort town on the east coast of the Yucatan Peninsula, just two hours from here. The Tulum ruins are the third most-visited archaeological site in Mexico, after Teotihuacan and Chichen Itza. This Maya archaeological site is situated on 12-metre tall cliffs which provide spectacular views over the Caribbean Sea. It was originally known by the name Zama meaning 'City of Dawn' because it faces the sunrise. The major structures of interest are El Castillo, the Temple of the Frescoes and the Temple of the Diving God."

My curiosity is instantly piqued.

"Did you say 'Diving God'?"

She nods sagaciously.

The guys are hooked.

When do we leave?

"Whenever."

I take the lead. We descend the steps together. Head to the bikes. Rosa climbs on behind me and slips her arms around my waist. Bernard extracts his original helmet. Plot the route on the GPS. Rev the engines.

I glance at my young friend. His energy seems discordant. Surely he is not jealous. Perhaps it is an issue with feminine energy. Hopefully he will process it during our final lesson.

Raise my hand and point to the open road.

The sacred ruins of Tulum are calling.

* * *

Bernard and I are sharing a room as usual. It's important to protect our camaraderie despite a gorgeous woman entering the scene. On top of that, Rosa is primarily our shaman so a little professional distance is in order. We are, of course, all in the same hotel.

Breakfast is delicious. I am trying to manage my beating heart, my friendship and the anticipation of our impending adventure. Consequently, I am not talking very much. Rosa suggests a visit to the archaeological site this morning. We readily agree.

Tulum is magnificent. Sapphire sky, viridescent grass, abundant trees, with a roped-off walkway ushering tourists through ancient ruins. Our first stop is the Temple of the Frescoes; we enter through the columns and admire the fine artwork. Bernard is enthralled.

The pathway gradually leads to El Castillo, standing about 7.5 metres high, with the smaller Temple of the Diving God to its left. We carefully climb the stone steps. The backdrop to both buildings is a palm-lined cliff overlooking the expansive Caribbean Sea. It's a breathtaking caress on the eyes. We briefly visit the Temple of the Diving God (aka Temple of the Descending God). A relief of the diving god is displayed above the entrance. A shiver runs down my back; curiously, it appears familiar.

We saunter down the wooden stairs to the gleaming white beach. The turquoise waters are irresistible. We strip down to our swimwear and plunge into the refreshing sea. There is much cavorting and splashing. Then we lay on the soft sand and soak up the sun.

Rosa repositions her towel so she is seated in front of us. She is wearing a lovely red sarong and her hair is curling around her face. There are very few tourists on the beach. Perhaps because it is almost Christmas; I guess most people are shopping.

She smiles cheerfully.

"It's time to bring more pleasure and love into your lives. You both have reasons for being isolated and alone. However, this is the moment of transition. The bridge to connect your worlds."

Unfastens her backpack. Reaches in, displays her open palm.

"Let me introduce you to a good friend."

Bernard scrutinises the brown bits.

Roughly granulated tree bark?

We all burst into laughter.

Then the lesson begins.

"The **cocoa** tree (*Theobroma 'food of the gods' cacao*) is native to the tropical regions of Central and South America. It grows in a narrow geographical zone measuring approximately 20 degrees to the north and south of the Equator. Interestingly, today nearly 70% of the world cocoa crop is grown in West Africa.

"There are three main varieties of cocoa trees: Forastero, Criollo and Trinitario. Forastero comprises 95% of the world production of cocoa. Criollo generates the highest quality cocoa; unfortunately it has lower yields and less resistance to cocoa tree diseases. Trinitario is a hybrid between Forastero and Criollo. It produces higher quality cocoa than Forastero yet has high yields and is more resistant to diseases.

"The fruit of the cocoa tree is a cocoa pod which has a rough and leathery rind about 2 cm thick. Each cocoa pod is filled with sweet gelatinous pulp encapsulating 30-50 soft seeds (cocoa 'beans') that appear pale lavender to deep purple.

"Cocoa beans are dried and fermented, then used to make cocoa powder, cocoa butter and chocolate, as well as many Mesoamerican foods such as mole sauce (generic name for a number of sauces used in Mexican cuisine) and tejate (a non-alcoholic maize and cocoa beverage traditionally made in Oaxaca).

"The most important product of cocoa beans is **raw chocolate** (aka raw cocoa). Raw chocolate is made by cold-pressing unroasted cocoa beans, a process that keeps the living enzymes in the cocoa and removes the fat (cocoa butter). This is vastly different to commercial chocolate that is often laden with harmful trans fats, hydrogenated oils, sugars and milk. Dairy, of course, contains lactose, a simple sugar that usually converts into fat in the human body.

"Raw chocolate is very healthy. Rich in minerals and potent antioxidants. Contains monoamine oxidase inhibitors (MAOIs) that improve mood because they allow serotonin and dopamine to remain in the bloodstream longer without being broken down (serotonin and dopamine are neurotransmitters which help alleviate depression and increase feelings of well-being). Also contains the mood-enhancing nutrients anandamide, phenethylamine and tryptophan."

Bernard puts on a singing voice.

Raw chocolate makes you feel good.

She bobs her head and grins.

"Considering your abstinence from alcohol, nicotine and caffeine, it is good to know there's raw chocolate. Here, try some."

Mmm ... slightly bitter ... pleasant taste.

My friend is grimacing.

It needs sugar.

Rosa glares at him.

"Sucrose, like lactose and fructose, converts into fat in your body. There are also a whole host of detrimental effects from the consumption of simple sugars. Do your research."

Sugar tickles the taste buds.

"Sugar is a recreational drug. Most people are addicted."

Tell us about healthy pleasures.

"Walks in nature, forests, oceans, mountains, sunrises and sunsets, scented baths, massages, deep sleep, music, art, reading, films, organic food, helping others, travelling, friendship, affection, sensuality, sexuality. And above all ... love."

I ponder the sand forlornly. We need more love.

Our shaman gives us a piercing gaze.

"You both have broken hearts. That is what drew you together. You have met higher beings, accessed the multi-dimensions, assimilated sacred teachings, experienced spiritual rebirth, and immersed in the Light. However, you have not healed your hearts."

She delves into her backpack. Extracts a handful of grey-green round cacti.

"**Peyote** is heart medicine. Prepare for your final journeys."

Bernard's face lights up immediately.

Teach us about this entheogen.

"Peyote (*Lophophora williamsii*) is a small spineless cactus containing psychoactive alkaloids, particularly **mescaline**. It is endemic to Mexico and south-western Texas. The name derives from the Nahuatl word peyotl (*pronounced pe-yacht*) meaning 'glisten' or 'glistening'. The top of the cactus, aka the crown, grows above ground and consists of disc-shaped buttons. The buttons are chewed (fresh or dried) or boiled in water to produce a psychoactive tea. Peyote is very bitter and often evokes nausea. Onset is usually within 45 minutes. The journey takes place during the day, mostly in nature, and lasts 6-8 hours depending on dosage. You experience brilliant colours, intense visions, dissolution of boundaries, deep insights and euphoria."

What are we waiting for?

"Indeed."

She passes a few buttons and we begin chewing. Ugh. Gnaw, munch, swallow, gnaw, munch, swallow. Just get it down. Wave of nausea hits me. Head between my legs.

Blackness engulfs me. Spinning. Loss of control.

Body morphing … seagulls flying … wings flapping within … thoughts and feathers … sun is sea is me … every grain is a world … hands merging into sand … rushing at, toward, engulfing … overwhelming azure … emerald breeze … one … one … one … pure hearts … swimming in loving eyes … freedom … abandon … melting … merging … chocolate hugs … no resistance … I am not alone … "Ha-ha-ha-ha-ha!" … I am not alone! … every detail revealed … nothing hidden … be real … be free … oh my …

"Whoo hoo!" ... eternal moment ... all is beautiful ... increasingly beautiful ... awesome ... incredible ... drowning in ecstasy ... kindred spirit ... "I see you!" ... "You see me!" ... no self ... one being ... one heart ... forever lovers ... One ... One ... One.

She is holding my hand ... on one side ... Bernard other side ... arm across his shoulders ... sun is setting ... "6.15pm" ... oh ... dazzling ... immense love and gratitude ... this is it ... why I am here ... why we are all here ... bring the Love ... shine the Light ... nothing more, nothing less ... radiant joy ... cascading peace ... integrate the higher dimensions into this world ... fold the sacred teachings into this reality ... here now ... here now.

Wow, dude. I'm not scared anymore.

"What's fear? I laugh at fear."

All three of us start giggling.

That was radical. Shifting geometric patterns, fabulous landscapes, jewelled architecture. Saw my divine nature ... and yours ... and yours. Shimmering resplendent souls travelling along golden rays of light. Then all pathways merged. No boundaries. One Path. One Heart. One Being. And you know what, brother?

I shake my head and smile.

Love is all that matters.

"I love you, bro!"

Love you too!

"The secret of your amazing journey?"

Same as every other journey.

"I'm listening."

Witness, breathe, surrender.

"The crucial one?"

Surrender.

"Amen."

* * *

We sleep deeply and restfully. Burdens lifted, fears dissipated, barriers shattered. Love and light flowing through our dreams. Tranquillity suffusing our souls.

Breakfast is granola, generously sprinkled with raw chocolate. Hmm. I will get used to this quickly. Even Bernard is adapting to the novel taste. The morning is spent enthusiastically discussing our peyote adventure.

At midday we ride to the beach below the sacred ruins. It's a marvellous place to journey. I breathe in the fresh invigorating air and survey the serene shore. Once again, there are hardly any people.

Unfurl our towels. Sit comfortably. Clear and seal the energy. Receive the peyote buttons. Chew, swallow, chew, swallow, chew, swallow.

Perhaps to take our minds off the nausea, Rosa asks a question.

"What is the nature of Love?"

Hmm … multilayered concept …

Love leads by example not by dictating.

I nod in agreement.

Love does not criticise or blame.

"Nice one, bro."

Love expresses needs openly.

Wow. He's rolling.

Love surrenders.

His pupils are di-la-ted.

Love walks its own path. Love is self-responsible.

Contemplating that for a moment.

Love does not depend on feelings. Empathy is a choice. Altruism is an action.

Oh my ... pink and gold vortex ... swirling in the sky ... subsuming me ... every sense magnified ... nothing I cannot see or hear ... endless details ... enhanced touch ... I am nature ... pulsing, rhythmic, alive ... networked ... neural pathways ... tree roots ... trunks ... branches ... leaves ... rain ... sun ... clouds ... insects ... birds ... animals ...

Breathe Love! Breathe Love!

Hairs on my arms bristling. Face is snarling. Something is wrong.

Bernard has bolted up the wooden stairs. Prancing along the rocks at the top.

We are the architects of Love! The architects of Love!

Bound up the steps. Pad along the cliff edge.

Watch him intently. Stones are scattering.

Foot slipping … losing its grip … everything slows … huge leap … grab his collar … too late … tumbling off the cliff … position myself under him … break his fall … loud yelp … not supposed to end this way … warm tears of blood … unable to move … hazy … indistinct … shimmer near the water …

The Crystal Shaman is walking toward me … young version … Am I dreaming? … Am I dead?

Peal of cryptic laughter pervades my consciousness.

"Really? Is that what you choose to believe?"

Sun beating down on me. Sand in mouth.

"Position dictates perception dictates reality."

Wha-a-a-t?

Suddenly aware of Bernard's screams.

No, no, no, no! Everyone I love dies.

The shaman whacks my leg.

Oh, that walking stick.

Bare my teeth.

Growl.

I am a point of consciousness. I manifest as I choose. All is consciousness. All is One Consciousness.

Memories rushing through my mind. Two greatest movers of the assemblage point are entheogens and intent … the rule … Faith guides intention; intention guides energy … wait … ah, yes … Intent is the prime mover … begins with a simple repeated command …

Sasha form … Sasha form … Sasha form … Sasha form … Sasha form … Sasha form!

Push away from the sand … shake my fur wildly … body shifting … eyes squinting … howling … grunting … "Oh, that's better."

Atlantean images bursting into my consciousness … white robe with blue mantle … leadership … tilt my head and gaze at the shaman … "Give me the sceptre … lessons learned … mastered Love … I have a mission to fulfil."

He hands me the gnarled walking stick. I invoke its true nature. The glorious Crystal Sceptre.

At last. My power returns.

I bow reverently to the young Atlantean.

"Thank you for protecting the sceptre. Thank you for keeping it safe. Revert to your rightful place as my second-in-command."

I scrutinise Bernard.

"My dear friend. What have you learned?"

He leaps into my arms and hugs me.

Sasha, you're alive! You're alive!

"What have you learned?"

To love in spite of pain and fear.

He reflects for a moment.

Dramas and issues belong to other people. Dramas seek company. Issues seek reinforcement. The secret is to walk the Path with quiet strength, clarity and purpose.

"What are you going to do?"

A broad smile lights up his face.

Return to San Francisco. Be with the woman I love. Become a clandestine shaman. Spread the advanced teachings. Share my star seed wisdom. Join the movement. Spark a revolution.

"Ah, the movement. Cosmic forces aligning with Earthly forces. Impending destruction of the dark lattice. Human race approaching an evolutionary jump. Imminent shift."

Indeed. The children of the stars will no longer walk alone on this Earth. Nor the Atlanteans and neo-Egyptians. The cosmic races, crystal people and stone people are uniting. The divine plan is unfolding. Change is coming.

We grip each other's forearms.

"Friends for life, brother."

Friends for life, brother.

Deep embrace.

He turns to the Crystal Shaman.

You aware of the date?

Good-natured smile.

"Christmas Eve."

Will you jump me home? Crystelle is waiting for me.

Flourish of the hand. Fractal vortex commencing.

Bernard presses his palms together and bows.

Place my fist on my heart.

"Love you, brother."

Love you too.

Hazy shimmer. They are gone.

Rosa reaches for my hand. We amble to the water's edge. The sky has turned maroon and gold. Sun is slowly dipping below the horizon. A soft breeze flutters the palms. Birds are murmuring and nuzzling in the cosy branches.

Our souls are exquisitely intermingling.

Love cascading through our beings.

A magnificent path lies ahead.

Stephen Shaw's Books

Visit the website: www.i-am-stephen-shaw.com

I Am contains spiritual and mystical teachings from enlightened masters that point the way to love, peace, bliss, freedom and spiritual awakening.

Heart Song takes you on a mystical adventure into creating your reality and manifesting your dreams, and reveals the secrets to attaining a fulfilled and joyful life.

They Walk Among Us is a love story spanning two realities. Explore the mystery of the angels. Discover the secrets of Love Whispering.

The Other Side explores the most fundamental question in each reality. What happens when the physical body dies? Where do you go? Expand your awareness. Journey deep into the Mystery.

Reflections offers mystical words for guidance, meditation and contemplation. Open the book anywhere and unwrap your daily inspiration.

5D is the Fifth Dimension. Discover ethereal doorways hidden in the fabric of space-time. Seek the advanced mystical teachings.

Star Child offers an exciting glimpse into the future on earth. The return of the gods and the advanced mystical teachings. And the ultimate battle of light versus darkness.

The Tribe expounds the joyful creation of new Earth. What happened after the legendary battle of Machu Picchu? What is Christ consciousness? Who are the 144,000?

The Fractal Key reveals the secrets of the shamans. This handbook for psychonauts discloses the techniques and practices used in psychedelic healing and transcendent journeys.

Lightning Source UK Ltd.
Milton Keynes UK
UKOW06f0306040216

267726UK00020B/536/P